Hotel Revolution

Published in Great Britain in 2005 by Wiley-Academy,
a division of John Wiley & Sons Ltd

Copyright © 2005

John Wiley & Sons Ltd, The Atrium, Southern Gate, Chichester, West Sussex, PO19
8SQ, England

Telephone (+44) 1243 779777

Email (for orders and customer service enquires): cs-books@wiley.co.uk

Visit our Home Page on www.wiley.co.uk or www.wiley.com

This publication is designed to provide accurate and authoritative information in regard
to the subject matter covered. It is sold on the understanding that the Publisher is not
engaged in rendering professional services. If professional advice or other expert
assistance is required, the services of a competent professional should be sought.

Other Wiley Editorial Offices

John Wiley & Sons Inc., 111 River Street, Hoboken, NJ 07030, USA

Jossey-Bass, 989 Market Street, San Francisco, CA 94103-1741, USA

Wiley-VCH Verlag GmbH, Boschstr. 12, D-69469 Weinheim, Germany

John Wiley & Sons Australia Ltd, 42 McDougall Street, Milton, Queensland 4064, Australia

John Wiley & Sons (Asia) Pte Ltd, 2 Clementi Loop #02-01, Jin Xing Distripark,
   Singapore 129809

John Wiley & Sons Canada Ltd, 22 Worcester Road, Etobicoke, Ontario,
   Canada M9W 1L1

ISBN-13 978 0 470 01680 0 (HB)

ISBN-10 0 470 01680 9 (HB)

Printed and bound by Conti Tipocolor, Italy

Hotel Revolution

Howard Watson

Series Designer **Liz Sephton**

contents

Executive Commissioning Editor: Helen Castle
Development Editor: Mariangela Palazzi-Williams
Design and Editorial Management: Famida Rasheed
Publishing Assistant: Louise Porter

For my parents

Acknowledgements

Many thanks to all the architects, designers, hoteliers, publicists, photographers and their teams who have contributed so much to this book – I apologise that there isn't enough space to thank you all by name. Particular thanks must go to Helen Castle, Famida Rasheed, Mariangela Palazzi-Williams and Louise Porter of Wiley-Academy, with whom it is a pleasure to work. The designer Liz Sephton has created another beautiful book, while the copy is indebted to the excellent editor Abigail Grater and proof-reader George Staines. I am very grateful to Luca Conte of Design Hotels, Gerard Greene, Matthew Falkiner, Richard Scott, Sofia de Meyer, Martin Hulbert, Ateliers Jean Nouvel, Philip Waterson, Christian Lacroix, Juliet de Valero Wills, John Pawson, Loock Hotels, Nigel Massey, Inez Voormolen, Weber Shandwick, Georgina Armstrong, Emily Davis, Jenny Thompson, Judi Wong, Suzy Ellis, Richard Dill, Kevin Farey, Ruth Gamper, Wilderness Safaris, Fiona Hamilton Andrews, Caroline Healey, MetroNaps, easyGroup, The Zetter, Boscolo Group, Neil Evans and, as ever, Miranda Harrison

Picture credits

Hotels have become galleries for conceptual art and lighting installations, their bars and restaurants are laboratories for the fulfilment of pleasure ... Hotels now provide an unbridled playground for design experimentation. The tag 'boutique' has been used to describe hotels that demonstrate a heightened exploration of design, but this is only a small part of the equation and distracts from the real, 21st-century adventures. 'Boutique', in the way the word is commonly used, should refer to a uniqueness of design, to the creation of a special, bespoke environment, but the concept has been watered down to the point that it is really a signifier of a uniform approach – perversely, boutique hotels are starting to look the same! Despite this, the cultural importance of hotel architecture and design has never been greater. Hotel Revolution focuses on the last five years, showing how the world's leading architects and designers have explored new ways to mirror, exemplify, or even initiate our changing sense of individual and cultural identity. Hotel designers have answered a clarion call for new concepts of luxury that reflect a modern diversity of needs, approaches and reflections. The designs are often spurred on by the restraints of modern city life. Some respond directly to the premium that is now placed upon space and location, while others focus on a combination of spatial and philosophical antidotes to our daily lives.

In recent years, our notion of luxury has changed. Encouraged by the media, we no longer perceive luxury as very remote or unattainable. In particular, hotels have entered a new level of exposure in the mainstream press. No longer the preserve of travel sections, hotel interiors are constantly featured in style magazines, newspaper supplements, television programmes and glossy

Introduction

magazines aimed at both the women's and men's markets. There has never been a period of such high design literacy (even if the translation of this new-found knowledge into home interiors is sometimes dyslexic). 'Lifestyle' has become the barometer of happiness for the ever-burgeoning design cognoscenti, and hotel design is now central to our aesthetic aspirations: hotels have become alluring places to eat and drink, while their interiors are seen as the height of novel, innovative design. Many hotels used to attempt to create 'a home from home'. For the most part, the order of things has been turned on its head. Increasingly, it seems that we want our homes to be luxurious like a hotel and this has led to a design democratisation as people try to recreate the look. This is understood by Kai Hollmann, owner of the budget-to-mid-price 25hours hotel in Hamburg: 'It's very important for 25hours that the consumer needs of trendsetters form part of the overall concept. Our target group wants to be able to buy what it likes immediately and without any problem.' Almost every product used in the interior design can be purchased at the reception.

At the same time, hotel architecture has become ever more culturally iconic and architects are being asked not just to design an environment for temporary accommodation, but to establish a landmark that will become a cultural identifier. In some ways, the Burj Al Arab in Dubai, which opened on the eve of the new millennium, kicked off the hotel revolution by demonstrating the full potential of hotel design. Shaped like a dhow on a man-made island, it remains the tallest single-use hotel building in the world. Its interior may be an exaggerated representation of luxurious Arabian hospitality, which is never going to appeal to refined minimalists, but the Burj redefined the Dubai emirate as an international player. It is *the* icon for Dubai's new-found status as a crucible for extreme wealth and luxury, and paved the way for the sanctioning of foreign property investment two years later. To some extent, many of the projects covered in this book highlight the extra-curricular, social and cultural importance of hotel design. Hotel Puerta América, involving a roster of the world's leading architects and designers, is a bold symbol of Madrid's attempt to regain confidence following the 2004 train bombings; Philippe Starck's Faena Hotel + Universe lets it be known that Argentina is back on its feet following a period of immensely destabilising hyper-inflation; Uma Paro is part of the Bhutan government's first step in attempting to initiate a controlled relationship with the West. In every case, the key to these hotels' success is the designers' capacity to combine innovation with cultural awareness at both a local and international level.

In many ways, the hotel revolution is rooted in a rediscovery and inspirational reinterpretation of the history of hotel culture, while at the same time absorbing the modern fragmentation of what makes up luxury. It can mean escape, serenity, location, or the endorsement of individuality or beliefs. The compression of city-space has led to the micro hotel – a bastardisation of the capsule hotel – which offers the luxury of location and the very best of technology at an affordable price, while the optimal conversion of existing spaces has become a major arena for innovation. The rigours of the city have also led to the rebirth of antidotes: the retreat, the spa and the country house hotel, where the prized luxuries are peace, health and relaxation. Meanwhile, ethical persuasions have given rise to the conscience resort, where designers have sought eco-friendly solutions without curtailing the pursuit of pleasure. Perhaps the ultimate luxury, which the boutique hotel originally did help to foster, is that of surprise, of the creation of the unique experience.

Below: **Whitepod, Villars.** Good design, exclusivity and zero-impact tourism are beginning to find common ground in new resorts such as Whitepod, where guests sleep in ecologically sound tents

The beginnings of hotel culture

The origin of hotel culture stretches back before the first permanent structures. In many ways, it begins with the tent: purpose-designed accommodation providing shelter in a temporary location. It may seem tenuous, but nomadic tribes can be seen as the forerunner to the modern international businessperson who sleeps in temporary accommodation, having travelled to new territories to seek some form of sustenance. There may be far more romance and spirituality associated with the former, but both require accommodation to suit the geographically temporary nature of their quests. In recent years, and away from the traditional campsite, the tent has entered a new era of design vogue. This is related to the explosion in eco-tourism, where the avoidance of permanent structures helps maintain delicate natural environments. Whitepod, the radical Swiss ski resort comprising Buckminster Fuller-style pods, provides a good example of a modern design solution that has its roots in both current ecological philosophy and the anthropology of the ancients.

Like the tent, the permanent hotel structure was created as a response to human mobility. The signposts of that mobility – ports, railways, highways, trading posts – all played a hugely important part in the foundation of the modern hotel. British hotel culture, which dates back to medieval times, grew up along the major highways between cities, with inns providing resting points for traveller and horse. The taverns and hotels of the East Coast of America met the demands of the huge waves of

Above: Tremont House, Boston. Opening in 1829, the Tremont established a mix of convenience, luxury and facilities that became the trademark of grand hotel culture

immigration of those seeking to carve out a future in the promised land, while the saloon-boarding houses of the Wild West grew alongside the frontier quest. The burgeoning of cities in the industrialised West gave rise to a huge mobility of labour and thus a new momentum for the metropolitan hotel, helped by the introduction of rail networks. Hotels continue to cluster around railway stations, which is an enduring reminder of the role of the hotel as a provider of temporary accommodation for those on an economic rather than leisure quest – utility and a quick exit are more important than the chance to become embroiled in the cultural heart of the city. It took a surprisingly long time for hotels to take on the mantle of purveyors of luxury for leisure time.

Foundations of luxury

The 'quest' lies at the heart of hotel culture. The quest may have originally been almost purely economic, but the 19th century saw a shift towards the sensory quest, towards travel purely for the sake of aesthetics and culture. The Industrial Revolution, with its creation of a wealthy middle class, mobility of labour and advanced travel networks, opened up the idea of cultural travel to a more significant number of people than the few aristocrats who would head off on the Grand Tour. This brought about a shift in the understanding of the role of the hotel. It was customary for the aristocratic classes of Europe, who were always more mobile than the poorer classes before the Industrial Revolution, to stay as the guest of another aristocratic family or to lease private houses if they did not have their own metropolitan residences. Entertainment was also largely private, taking the form of soirees, dinners, balls and visits to private clubs, which were based upon the interiors of domestic residences. In broad terms, although it did appeal to the upper echelons, the grand hotel was a social innovation that met the needs of a new, affluent middle class which was creating the modern concept of refined public leisure and tourism. Although the Industrial Revolution began in Britain towards the end of the 18th century, the finest example of its effect on hotel culture, and its connection to contemporary concepts of luxury, is found in the United States.

Tremont House in Boston, built by Isaiah Rogers in 1829, is not only famous for Charles Dickens's description of it in his *American Notes* 13 years later: rightly, it is often cited as one of the most important buildings in hotel history. This importance lies not only in its display of luxury, but also in how that sense of luxury was linked to innovation. With a neo-classical exterior, large, high-ceilinged public spaces, fine upholstery, bellhops and complimentary toiletries, the Tremont helped create the model for the grand hotel. However, some of the most-loved luxuries were its use of recent innovations such as plumbing and a simple prototype of the telephone that guests could use to contact reception. Reputedly, it was the first hotel in the United States to guarantee private rooms rather than asking guests to share with others. Not only that, guests had the key to their rooms, giving them the independence to come and go as they pleased. These were the seeds for a respect for individualism that has become a mainstay of hotel culture and is connected to the burgeoning, anti-homogenous design concepts that snowballed during the 'boutique' years.

Left: **Savoy, London.** Richard D'Oyly Carte opened the Savoy in 1889, partly to provide accommodation for Gilbert and Sullivan devotees attending operettas at his theatre

Below: **The Ritz, London.** César Ritz was an early exponent of the idea of a luxury brand, with both the Paris and London hotels bearing his name

Below: **The Ritz, London.** From the Tremont to YOtel, innovation has been the hallmark of good hotel design. The Ritz London, which opened in 1906, is one of London's most significant early steel-frame structures

Grand hotel culture reached Europe later in the 19th century, with the Savoy opening in London in 1889 and The Ritz Paris opening in 1898. Like the Tremont, innovative architecture and design could be found amongst the purveyance of luxury. The 1906 Ritz London was one of the city's first significant steel-framed buildings and also introduced the concept of individual bathroom facilities. Furthermore, the new hotels reflected the change in social culture, offering grand public spaces, bars and restaurants which became a destination in themselves, something that is mirrored in the recent rebirth of the hotel as a dynamic social space.

The corporate brand

Travelling salesmen have played an important part in the development of the hotel ever since their emergence in the early days of the Industrial Revolution. During the 19th century, as modern hotel culture began to find its feet, they dominated the clientele, consistently taking up the majority of rooms in larger metropolitan hotels. This was especially true in the United States, where salesmen explored a vast terrain in search of commercial opportunities. National chains such as Hilton and Statler were already appearing in the first half of the 20th century, responding to a need for travellers to feel comfortable with a certain level of facilities and service wherever their business took them. This need was married with advances in manufacturing and the building trade that not only enabled the standardisation of architecture, interiors and services, but also gave the benefit of economies of scale. It was quickly realised that it is far cheaper to mass-produce one carpet pattern for 100 hotels than to seek bespoke designs for individual properties. Chains were able to associate their names with a level of quality that assured the business traveller that there would be at least one known factor as they stepped into unknown territory. Of course, the tremendous globalisation of industry in the second half of the 20th century moved the concept of the national chain into the international arena, with chains such as

Hilton, with US coast-to-coast experience of branding and standardisation, setting the standard. Corporate philosophy dominated hotel design, expanding hand-in-hand with both the globalisation of business and the rapid growth of the tourist market.

It was not only business travellers who were happy with the standardisation of accommodation. Branding lay at the heart of grand hotel culture from the outset – it wasn't a lack of imagination that led César Ritz to give his Paris and London hotels the same name. As cultural tourists explored new cities and foreign lands, many revelled in the securities of the brand, the daily fresh white towels and the 'safe' restaurant menu. However, the advances of the 20th century created a duplicitous cultural landscape which was to have an enormous effect on contemporary hotel culture. At the same time as metropolitan environments have become more homogenised, the cult of the individual has become rampant. Everybody wants the same thing: everybody wants to be different.

When small means big: the rise of the boutique

The rise of the corporate chain was only part of the progress of 20th-century hotel design, which saw the emergence of many types of hotel from spas and eco-resorts to capsule hotels, meeting the diverse needs of modern lifestyles. However, it was a reaction to corporatism in the form of the 'boutique hotel' that dominated hotel design, or at least its media coverage, in the final years of the century.

The late 20th century has seen a significant change in people's relationship with their architectural surroundings. The number of people who can be regarded as design-savvy has grown exponentially, both affected by and affecting so many aspects of contemporary culture from the way couture is marketed and sold, the profile of bar and restaurant design, and the type of television and film content, to the expectations of public architecture and so on. Modernism and the Machine Age had progressed to offer freedom of opportunity in terms of standardisation but the Information Age has helped give a broad base of people access to specific knowledge. The cognoscenti are growing in number, and none of them wants to feel like a cog on a wheel. They demand environments that allow their sense of individuality to blossom, rather than to shrivel within the bounds of metropolitan conformity. The boutique

Right: Chicago Hilton & Towers, Chicago.
Conrad Hilton took a significant step towards world domination in 1945 when he bought the Stevens, then the largest hotel in the world, and turned it into a Hilton

answered an existing demand, but soon engendered new design expectations amongst an even greater number of people. In contrast to a growing impersonality of service and homogeneity of high-street design, the boutique allowed the clientele to think, 'The hotel's unique and I'm unique, too.' This reflection offers a new concept of luxury beyond the provision of services and the quality of materials.

Ian Schrager and Steve Rubell, known for having their finger on the pulse through the ultra-hip 1970s nightclub Studio 54, christened the 'boutique' genre when they opened Morgans in the mid-1980s, but even they could not have guessed at the size of the monster they helped create. Many hotels that fit the boutique genre, such as Anouska Hempel's Blakes in London, opened well before the term entered common parlance and the definition of boutique remains chameleon. Of course, the word carries a sense of being small, originally referring to a small shop or business selling items such as clothes or jewellery. It conveys a suggestion of quality, that the items are perhaps crafted, limited edition, or even bespoke, and certainly luxurious and fashionable. Its translation into hotel culture is at best a little garbled. Some people claim that Schrager's own hotels, which have several hundred rooms, are not boutique – after all, how small is small? I think Schrager meant that the hotel should evoke a personal relationship with the guest, offering him/her a unique and surprising experience which cannot be exactly repeated in any other environment. Schrager is very good at presenting new concepts, and following them through in a physical form. Aided by the radicalism of designer Philippe Starck, he set a high benchmark, and consequently expectations of boutique culture continue to be lofty.

In *Locum Destination Review*, Mark Lomanno of Smith Travel Research tried to create a balance between tangible and intangible elements when he described the boundaries of the boutique hotel genre as, to paraphrase: appealing to leisure and business travellers, especially women; mostly

Above: **Hilton Olympia, London.** Hilton has become synonymous with corporate branding. The chain offers assurances of a certain level of quality, but this understanding of luxury has been somewhat superseded by a quest for consumer individuality

Above: **Morgans, New York.** Ian Schrager and Steve Rubell christened the boutique genre when they opened Morgans, designed by Andrée Putman, in New York in 1985

Above: **Blakes, London.** The late 20th century saw hotel interiors begin to make a significant impact on individual lifestyle choices. Blakes' tall black standard lamps are available from Anouska Hempel's 'Pour la Maison' range

Left: **Blakes, London.** Blakes (1981) was one of the first hotel designs that could be described as 'boutique'. The interior of Blakes addresses a rampant mix of styles and influences through a series of individually designed rooms

Right and below: **W, Los Angeles.** The idea of the boutique hotel was to provide a bespoke alternative to the branded, corporate chain. However, the successful W chain (a brand of one of the world's largest hotel companies) has managed to merge the genres

containing between 150 and 200 rooms although the bracket stretches to include those with as few as 50 rooms and as many as 400; offering a homely atmosphere, personalised service, distinctive style and generous amenities; and all-importantly, for the more sophisticated traveller, they are 'the right place to stay'. As the boutique concept flirts with an emotional interplay between hotel and customer, entering the realms of the philosophical, the psychological and the intangible, no definition can be finite. The grey areas have led to its commercial abuse. 'Boutique' has been co-opted by every manner of hotelier to the point that it no longer has much to do with presenting a design philosophy: it is all too easily used as a way to cut corners to make a quick buck, riding on the commercial benefits of the genre's popularity. And the benefits are great. Smith Travel Research's figures show that in the US, the boutique sector is the genre with the highest performance, with increasing yields. Because 'boutique' carries with it an idea of luxury and uniqueness, room rates are high. Catching onto this benefit, existing hotels began to call themselves 'boutique' without so much as moving the furniture, while the design of new ones sometimes has very little to do with high concepts or uniqueness.

Rather than offering a genuinely innovate interplay between building and guest, 'boutique' has become a devalued currency and is little different than corporatism: it is now more to do with using a 'brand' for which the hotel doesn't even have to pay. The hotels lure the customer, promising a fitting setting for their individualism, but on inspection many boutiques are merely using devices, such as a piece of shocking contemporary art, to hide the absence of real design innovation. When you try to look at the real substance, you realise that in many cases the relationship between hotel and guest has become plagued with kidology. A hotel with a thoroughly mundane design, with the exception of a single oversized and unusual floor lamp in the middle of the foyer, now markets itself as 'boutique'. At another a massive Buddha introduces a design which in no other way purveys the ethics of Buddhism: welcome to the boutique experience. In countless more, rooms are fitted out with an indiscriminate hotchpotch of items seemingly bought as a job lot at a car-boot sale – this is an 'eclectic, boutique style'. Sometimes, the media seems to be complicit in failing to expose the designs as lazy, incoherent pastiches. Then, to cap it all with a final irony, branded chains became 'boutique'. W, the often-lauded design hotel chain, is part of the same group as Westin, exactly the sort of hotel that had become despised by the new breed of hotel guest. Starwood, the owner of both, cannot be blamed: it has just read the market well, and dressed its corporatism in different accessories. One must acknowledge that the W designs are successful, yet at the same time they are not 'boutique-unique': they may have different designers but they share an identifiable design style, a brand that goes beyond names and logos. Starwood has successfully played it both ways, combining a demand for high design with the securities of the chain. Meanwhile,

Hilton has also dipped its toe in the boutique market with the Trafalgar in London, and Le Meridien is going global with an 'Art and Tech' room concept.

The boutique hotel should provide an oasis from contemporary design homogeneity, but, on the whole, the genre has conjured a very modern vapidity. However, there have been genuine benefits of boutique culture. Amongst the charlatans, certain designers brought a quality of execution and detail that was innovative, while interacting with the customer in a personal way that was ground-breaking. Perhaps best of all, good boutique hotels have raised the profile and expectations of hotel design. It is a shame, though, that while the column inches have been so dominated by indiscriminate explorations of boutique culture over the last decade, it seems to have gone largely unnoticed in the mainstream media that there is a real hotel revolution going on, which truly does respond to the freedoms and constraints of the modern metropolitan lifestyle with innovative design.

New realities

It may have its roots in previous centuries, but there is a new focus on the way that hotel design can offer possibilities of personal fulfilment. This is the real skill, rather than pretending to offer something genuinely unique through the careless tipping out of second-hand furniture into boxy rooms. Free from the chains of corporatism, and the devices that have become the signature of the boutique, designers can use the hotel to explore innovative responses to the modern lifestyle, or rather, to counteract the failures of its reality.

For all the sexiness of the word 'boutique', it is the more prosaic-sounding genres of 'eco-resort', 'micro-hotel', 'budget' and 'spa' that are inspiring some of the world's leading designers and architects to create revolutionary, and often very sensual, solutions for modern life. This book traces the evolution of these genres into distinctive 21st-century design, while also giving space to radical solutions that defy categorisation.

The capsule hotel, which emerged in 1970s Japan as a solution to metropolitan overcrowding, is now being reborn in the West through micro-solutions such as YOtel, which combines technological innovation and aircraft

Above: **Capsule hotel, Tokyo.** Established in the 1970s, Japanese capsule hotels take the hotel concept to its bare minimum, stacking coffin-size units on-end

Above: **MetroNaps, New York.** Individual sleeping pods can be placed within office blocks and airports to provide a powernap facility for time-poor workers and travellers

Left: **YOtel, prototype.** The YOtel concept aims to offer a low-budget, inner-city solution, drawing on capsule hotels and airline cabins to offer high design in a confined space

Above: Bleibtreu, Berlin. While eco-resorts started to spring up in South America and Africa in the 1970s, it took until the late 1990s for European hoteliers to really display their ecological credentials. At the Bleibtreu, which opened in 1995, almost everything from the paint and furniture to the food is made to high, eco-friendly standards

cabin design to give a low-budget, high-design response to metropolitan overcrowding. It distils the luxuries of good design and location, as does MetroNaps, which places sleeping pods in office blocks and airports, radically evolving hotel concepts into techno-capsules for powernaps. Other leading designers are lending their creativity to this luxury of location through the democratisation of high design, offering inner-city, low-budget solutions, or are responding to the evolution of economic needs and lifestyles through the optimal conversion of redundant spaces.

While many designers deal with the compression of the city from within its walls, others lend their creativity to the burgeoning need for antidotes to the metropolis. It seems that, in increasing numbers, we need a valve to release the pressure of city life. This release is psychological, and some would say philosophical or spiritual, as well as spatial. Alongside the new English country house retreats, which combine historical architecture, contemporary interiors and spa facilities, a new breed of spa hotel has emerged as an international, serene solution to the ultra-speed and psychological compression of metropolitan life. Like the better-designed boutique hotels, these spas provide a release from the homogeneity of contemporary environments and redress the dominance of automation. It is almost as if we were increasingly relying on hotel culture to represent a true idea of our individuality. This also relates to the rise of the eco-resort, which is now entering a design renaissance through the work of the likes of Matteo Thun. It offers a political antidote to the rigours and destructiveness of urbanity. Taking a vacation from be-suited workdom, the guests become devout eco-warriors, who are at one with themselves and nature, and consequently have a rather more impressive idea of themselves as individuals. We have entered a new era where the design of these eco-resorts uses natural materials and responsible technology to match the heightened expectations of the clientele.

The pressure for the hotel to deliver spatial, philosophical and culturally iconic solutions has never been higher but this has invigorated many designers. They have responded by truly stretching the boundaries of hotel culture, presenting diverse concepts of luxury in revolutionary ways. The designers who succeed most are the ones who best understand the needs and aspirations of the guests, while conjuring aesthetic surprises that still give a tremor to even the most ardent of style cognoscente. *Hotel Revolution* is a celebration of their work.

Right: Vigilius, South Tyrol. Matteo Thun's Vigilius Mountain Resort, which is accessible only by cable car, signposts a new era where high design and high ethics can be combined for a luxurious experience

shock

The need to shock – or at least surprise – has become part and parcel of contemporary hotel design. Bizarrely, people have come to expect it. This is partially the legacy of the boutique hotel where so much emphasis is placed on a personal interplay between environment and guest. Ian Schrager calls the relationship that designer Philippe Starck wishes to initiate as 'hotel as theatre' and talks of 'access to new experiences' as the modern luxury. In boutique terms, this often relies on unusual juxtapositions and the positioning of undersized, oversized or 'artistic' objects in surprising places. In the wrong hands, or in an unresolved interior, this can come across as shallow or just plain crass. Essentially, the requirement to surprise lies at the heart of so much poor, overrated, sub-Starckesque boutique design. But fear not. There is a raft of architects and designers who are unmoved by the painting-by-numbers approach to hotel design. They are simultaneously exploring the relationship between a building and its macro-environment, and the relationship between the building and its residents, while establishing new boundaries. Their approaches are refreshing and individual – this is not a 'movement' but a chaos of singular personalities whose paths criss-cross to give a new texture to hotel culture.

In recent decades, the cult of the individual has reigned supreme at the consumer end of hotel design. The customer must be made to feel special; the homogenous, automaton aspects of everyday life are pushed to one side once they enter the hotel bubble. The projects in this chapter highlight how this has been achieved, but also show that the personal innovation of designers is the all-important starting point. 2005 saw the opening of two collective hotel showpieces – New York's Hotel on Rivington and Madrid's

shock

Hotel Puerta América. Each involves a selection of the world's most famous designers, but they are not working together to create some sort of superbrand. Each designer works on their individual floor or amenity, with little or no reference to an overall design theme. As a result, we have a lobby that delights in one way, and a guestroom that delights in another. Rather than a hotchpotch, the variety of moods and materials can create a successful, invigorating play on the senses and emotions, and takes into account the design literacy of the guest who does not wish to be anaesthetised by a seamless, corporate identity.

A vibrant cross-ethnicity is flavouring hotel culture with unbridled, undiluted arias. More and more new hotels have iconic status. The Burj Al Arab, which appears to sail the seas in a physical embodiment of man's dextrous power, is the new symbol of Dubai. The facade of Hotel Puerta América tells the world that Madrid will not be cowed by terrorism, while the Hotel on Rivington announces that the Lower East Side of New York is the new hub of Manhattan. However, the designers of these new expressions of city culture are invariably outsiders who are adding a new dynamic to the social fabric. Hotel culture is all about luxury, but the way of achieving it has splintered. The creation of the cocoon is often central to the intention of the interior design, but while the Burj creates this with layers of traditional ostentation and splendour, the designers of many of these hotels are articulating luxury through a new relationship with materials. Q! in Berlin takes the idea of the luxurious cocoon to the extreme, but does this by using Marmoleum, a flexible innovation based on linoleum. Meanwhile, at the Semiramis, Karim Rashid reawakens the relationship with everyday objects by using coloured, translucent materials; and Marcel Wanders introduces the Hotel on Rivington's lobby-cocoon, made out of foam coated with fibreglass-reinforced concrete, with a snowflake pattern of Bisazza mosaic tiles.

The hotel revolution is both textural and contextual. Each design is individual, innovatively creating a new relationship between guests, culture and the built environment, while simultaneously asking questions, demanding reactions, and offering comforts. Hotel design is entering a new era of diversity, nourishing our desire to be shocked and surprised in an increasingly emotionally immune world.

Below: **Semiramis, Athens**. The entranceway from the bar into the double-height lounge is a cutout in the translucent orange wall. Inside, the seating includes Karim Rashid's 'Spline' chairs and sofas

Burj Al Arab

WS Atkins & Partners/KCA International

Location: **Dubai**
Completion date: **1999**

When the Burj Al Arab, which remains the tallest single-use hotel building in the world, opened on the eve of the millennium, it seemed that the use of iconic architecture for hotels had reached its apex. Furthermore, inside the hotel, traditional concepts of luxury were pushed to their furthest, most ornate boundaries. To reflect this, the hotel even awarded itself hitherto unknown seven-star status. Of course, some critics reacted with horror: it had all gone too far. Whatever the opinion of onlookers, the Burj is one of the most important buildings in the recent history of Dubai and shows how hotel design can have a fulsome effect on a city or state's relationship with the outside world. With Frank O Gehry's signature architecture, the Guggenheim Museum brought what is now referred to as 'the Bilbao effect' to northern Spain – the Burj's 'Dubai effect' dwarfs it in terms of financial and cultural implications. As a result of its international success, the United Arab Emirates has become a magnet for Middle Eastern tourism and the playground for outrageous hotel design.

The hotel name alone – the Tower of Arabs – shows how much the endeavour is connected to cultural identity. It was a statement to the world, showcasing Arabian achievement and the booming Emirate city-states that have emerged out of the desert since the 1970s. Burj Al Arab is a 321-metre-high tower, shaped like a sail, that stands proudly on the water off the Jumeirah Beach: having conquered the desert, the Arabs demonstrated that they could conquer the sea. Some may think the concept brash, but the hotel stands as a testament to man's harnessing of nature. The exterior architecture itself, though, is not brash. It is tall and surprising, but also really quite sublime as it arcs its way up towards the sky. From the outside, one could believe that it is a temple to minimalism. It isn't.

The Burj houses some of the most excessive interiors of the modern world. It has walls covered with gold leaf, solid gold bathroom fittings, multi-coloured pillars, Arabian carpets and a mass of marble. It places the greatest excesses of French baroque within a Middle Eastern bazaar of geometric patterns. If the architecture expresses that it cannot be restrained by nature, then the interior shows that it is not restrained by anything at all. It is the full stop to traditional pursuits of luxury that have become the trademark of grand hotels since the Victorian era: plushness, ornateness, comfort and service are taken to their ultimate conclusion. Even the marketing is beyond conventional bounds: Andre Agassi and Roger Federer are brought in to play tennis on the heliport, which cantilevers over the sea; Tiger Woods tees off on the same spot to send his golf ball far off into the waves. Its ostentation knows no bounds. It's a minimalist's nightmare. It's hugely successful.

Jumeirah Beach is now awash with new luxury hotels, some of which bear impressive architecture that would

Above: **Burj Al Arab, Dubai.** At 321 metres high, this is the world's tallest hotel. Despite that, the exterior (which features a cantilevered heliport towards the top) is relatively restrained compared to the interior

Opposite: **Burj Al Arab, Dubai.** The hotel, standing like a sail braced against the wind, forms its own island in the sea off Jumeirah Beach

Hotel name	Burj Al Arab
Address	PO Box 74147, Dubai, United Arab Emirates
Telephone	+971 4 301 7777
Website	www.burj-al-arab.com
Design style	Unadulterated decadence in a sail-shaped exterior
No. of rooms	202 suites
Bars and restaurants	Al Muntaha (European); Al Mahara (seafood); Al Iwan (Middle Eastern); Majlis Al Bahar (Mediterranean); Juna Lounge cocktail bar; Sahn Eddar lounge; Skyview Bar; Bab Al Yam café
Spa facilities	Assawan Spa & Health Club: 2 gyms; 2 swimming pools (1 women-only); sauna, steam room & plunge pool; 2 Jacuzzis; squash court; 2 solariums; fitness studio. Wide range of massages, facial and body treatments, including Ayurvedic
Clientele	Super-rich jetsetters with a penchant for 'more is more'

be taken more seriously if the United Arab Emirates wasn't so casually dismissed by some critics as a Disneyland for design. Jumeirah International, owners of the Burj, is responsible for two of the most interesting: Emirates Towers is made up of two skyscraper shards which would have some other cities cooing about their great modern architecture, while the earlier Jumeirah Beach Hotel is a breaking wave upon the shorefront.

Meanwhile, the government of Dubai's Emirate neighbour, Abu Dhabi, has reportedly spent £2 billion dollars to take the title of the world's plushest hotel with the Emirates Palace. A traditional-style, outsized palace complex featuring 114 domes, it took 20,000 people three years to build it from scratch. It doubles up as a new national monument – such has been the journey for iconic hotel architecture.

The Emirates' hotel adventure doesn't stop there. Opposite Jumeirah Beach, two artificial, palm-shaped islands are being created, forging 120 square kilometres of new land out of the sea. In time, The Palms will be home to 80 new hotels. Before that's completed, Dubai will also have the Hydropolis, a semi-submerged, 220-suite hotel which will feature an auditorium housed in a translucent dome rising out of the sea.

Left: Emirates Towers, Dubai. Jumeirah International's Emirates Towers opened in 2000, shortly after the Burj

Opposite: Burj Al Arab, Dubai. The 180-metre lobby atrium, where one of the world's most ostentatious interiors begins to reveal itself on the ground floor

Below: Jumeirah Beach Hotel, Dubai. Inspired by Arabic seafaring tradition, the 1997 Beach Hotel is a breaking wave on the shorefront

Opposite: **Burj Al Arab, Dubai.** The journey to the award-winning, underwater Al Mahara Restaurant begins with a short, simulated submarine ride. Diners look into a central seawater aquarium

Below: **Burj Al Arab, Dubai.** The lobby's outsized, S-shaped double divan could be at home in a Starck-designed hotel atrium. This being the Burj, it bears a gold motif

Opposite, above: Burj Al Arab, Dubai. The Royal Suite living room is a paean to unbridled ostentation. The maze of gold leaf, geometric patterns, drapes and cushions could give rise to sensory overload

Opposite, below: Burj Al Arab, Dubai. Versailles seems minimalist compared to the Royal Suite's marble and gold bathroom

Above: Burj Al Arab, Dubai. The bedroom of the Royal Suite, with the four-poster bed raised on a circular dais

Right: Burj Al Arab, Dubai. The indoor pool in the Assawan Spa & Health Club is awash with geometric patterns

Hotel Puerta América

Jean Nouvel et al

Location: **Madrid**
Completion date: **2005**

Foster, Hadid, Chipperfield, Gluckman, Pawson and Arad all working on the same building? The Silken Group certainly doesn't lack ambition. It has invested 75 million euros and hired 18 of the world's leading architects and designers to create an iconic 360-room hotel for Madrid. The Group's president claims that Hotel Puerta América is 'a project where acclaimed architects and designers have conveyed their dreams to us. It is a homage to the world of architecture, design and to freedom.' Rarely is quite so much expectation placed upon a commercially financed project, but the reasons go beyond the cast of superstar architects and the level of investment. The word 'freedom' is not used glibly: the hotel plays a very demonstrative part in Madrid's rehabilitation after the terrible rail bombings of 2004. That year was meant to be a milestone in the city's tourism, following massive investment in its major museums. Madrid has long lagged behind Barcelona in terms of both significant architecture and self-promotion, and has appeared to be ignorant of the hotel design renaissance that has helped re-energise tourism in many European cities. At the point at which Madrid was finally awakening, the rail-bombings put it in trauma. Puerta América isn't just a place for the daydreams of architects and night-dreams of residents: it has the frightening responsibility of being a highly publicised crucible for a city's rebirth.

Silken calls Puerta América the first multicultural hotel project in

Spain, with designers originating from both Americas, Asia, Australia and all over Europe. It's a who's who of modern architecture, and with different designers for each of the 12 storeys, it is inevitably a dictionary of different styles. In fact, Silken was not seeking any cohesion between the floor designs, asking the designers not to talk to each other. Apart from dealing with so many distinctive egos (surely one of the most formidable tasks in the history of project management), one of the main tasks was to create a meaningful box for such a compendium. Jean Nouvel designed the exterior, and he chose to address directly the principal themes of internationalism and freedom. The facade is made up of blocks of colour, rising up through orange to yellow, and down to deep terracotta and purple. These coloured panels are studded with excerpts from Paul Eluard's poem 'Liberty', written in many languages including French, English, Chinese and Arabic (thereby holding a memory of the Islamic use of calligraphy) – freedom, democracy and inclusiveness are ingrained in the design.

Inside, Puerta América is a hotchpotch, but the problem is lessened by using the arch-minimalist John Pawson to design the communal areas, thereby creating a passive backdrop to the chaos of themes that inhabit the rooms on different floors. A few architecture critics have claimed that some of the more famous contributors, have merely placed

Above: Hotel Puerta América, Madrid. Jean Nouvel's exterior for Hotel Puerta América features a multi-coloured array of panels inscribed with extracts from 'Liberty', a poem by Paul Eluard, in various languages

Opposite: Hotel Puerta América, Madrid. The hotel has 12 storeys with Zaha Hadid, Norman Foster, David Chipperfield, Plasma, Victorio & Lucchino, Marc Newson, Ron Arad, Kathryn Findlay, Gluckman Mayner, Arata Izozaki, Javier Mariscal and Jean Nouvel each designing a floor

Hotel name	Hotel Puerta América
Address	Avenida de América 41, Madrid 28002, Spain
Telephone	+34 902 363 600
Website	www.hotelpuertamerica.com
Design style	Playbox for the world's superstar designers
No. of rooms	342 rooms
Bars and restaurants	Restaurant; bar
Spa facilities	Spa services, gym & rooftop swimming pool
Clientele	Big-brand-loving design cognoscenti

their signature style within a hotel context. It seems that if the hotel conveys the designers' dreams, then some critics can only wish insomnia upon them. Having so many contributors, it is difficult to like everything about Puerta América, but by the same token, it is hard not find many things that are delightful. It is refreshing that it is some of the lesser-known contributors that have teased out innovation amongst the company of giants.

Eva Castro and Holger Kehne of London-based Plasma Studio, for instance, have thrown the book out of the window, breaking down the typical linearity of hotel structures by creating a fourth-floor corridor with a stainless-steel skin that contorts along angular planes and fractures according to its own rhythm. The steel reflects seams of coloured light that change along the course of the corridor and identify a zonal colour code that seeps into the rooms. The floor is not a comfort zone, but rather a realignment of identity in a surreal, non-repetitive space. On the eighth floor, designed by Kathryn Findlay, British lighting designer Jason Bruges offers another invigorating idea of identity within the hotel space. The corridor walls

are lined with sensors that trace the guests' movements. The images are then absorbed and edited to form a shadow play that develops through the course of the day: the guests become part of the hotel design.

Some of the old masters have also stepped up to the challenge, particularly Ron Arad whose seventh-floor rooms feature a central, flowing mass that belches out the utilities and removes the need for internal barriers. Even if the work of other contributors is unlikely to be classed as experimental, it will still be fresh to most of the guests as they are unlikely to have experienced the signature style of the likes of Pawson and Foster within a more-or-less domestic setting.

From different viewpoints, it is easy to be embarrassed by the way Puerta América literally wears its heart on its sleeve or to be tempted to write it off as a huge marketing ploy. Nevertheless, amongst all the philosophical extemporising, it does follow through its intent to stand tall for democratic, inclusive principles, and amongst the sensational publicity, there are many innovative design gems to behold.

Above: Hotel Puerta América, Madrid. Zaha Hadid has used her signature fluid forms in creating a series of virtually monochrome room designs

Opposite: Hotel Puerta América, Madrid. Eva Castro and Holger Kehne of Plasma have integrated fractured planes and coloured neon to subvert the expectations and regimentation of hotel corridor and room design

Right: Hotel Puerta América, Madrid. David Chipperfield's design for the rooms on the third floor features black terracotta flooring and an enclosing canopy

Above left: Hotel Puerta América, Madrid. In Ron Arad's seventh floor design, all the elements, including the bathroom fittings, flow from a central, curvaceous mass

Left: Hotel Puerta América, Madrid. Partially inspired by the Spanish artist Eduardo Chillida, Norman Foster set out to create 'a contrast from the busy, urban world of the city outside'. He was drawn to the project by the use of different designers, promising 'variety, when a hotel is normally anonymous'.

Above: Hotel Puerta América, Madrid. The
corridor and lift area of the eighth floor, designed by
Kathryn Findlay in collaboration with Jason Bruges

Above: **Hotel Puerta América, Madrid.** Overall, the disparate floor designs are linked by a leaning towards interpretations of minimalism, but maximalists have their own den in Victorio & Lucchino's fifth floor

Below: **Hotel Puerta América, Madrid.** The 11th floor is designed by Spaniards Javier Mariscal and Fernando Salas, who also designed Silken Hotels' acclaimed Gran Hotel Domine in Bilbao

Above: Hotel Puerta América, Madrid. Australian Marc Newson, famous for his furniture and household objects, has designed both the bar and the sixth floor

Left and below: Hotel Puerta América, Madrid. With an emphasis on stone and blond wood, the foyer is designed by John Pawson to be a curving, cloister-like space

Semiramis
Karim Rashid

Location: **Athens**
Completion date: **2004**

Karim Rashid, the industrial designer, is famous for giving a fresh twist to the design of domestic objects but recently he has widened the parameters of his vision to alter our perception of the hotel. His first completed project, which he has called a '21st-century creation', abandons the retro concepts that have dominated recent hotel design in favour of a bright new world of surprising colours and materials. He has also used contemporary art to make sure that this hotel is very far away from the concept of a 'home from home'.

The entrance to the hotel is a bright glass cube – a pink lightbox which suggests that the guest is an outsider studying an artistic creation. Indeed, the lobby acts as an exhibition space for artworks that are on loan from major galleries as well as the collection of Dakis Joannou, Semiramis' owner. Joannou has invested 23 million euros in a hotel that has just 52 rooms (including six poolside bungalows, three penthouse studios and one penthouse suite), so Rashid's creation is under pressure to lure a lucre-heavy clientele who are willing to pay for good design.

The use of translucent, coloured glass is a feature throughout the hotel rooms, from the balconies that adorn the white facade to orange shower screens and blue basins. The effect is to bring a light modernity and fun to the whole design. A curving, opaque glass wall provides some privacy in the bathroom but does not detract from the openness of the space, and allows more light into the main room. Almost all the furniture is lifted on steel legs, while there are virtually no closed-off cupboards. The art-and-light concept that greets the guest at the entrance is also prevalent here, with a backlit artwork from Rashid's 'digipop' series of images hanging above the bed. These digipop symbols are also used to identify individual rooms, rather than numbers. The wish to break away from standard systems of communication is taken further in the pool bungalows, where guests can scroll electronic messages, such as 'Privacy', across

their doors at the touch of a button. Modern technology is also emphasised throughout the rooms, with flat and plasma television screens, CD, DVD and internet access, cordless headsets, remote control curtains, and so on.

Rashid is an astonishingly successful self-publicist, forever ready with killer quotes to advertise his own radicalism, and he has taken the opportunity to exhibit a wide range of his own designs within Semiramis. The guestrooms are full of his creations, including 'Swing' chairs in the penthouses, although they are augmented by a few works by other shining lights such as Marc Newson. The restaurant area includes Rashid's 'Kab' chairs alongside tables whose morphotic shape – like an amoeba about to divide into two – allows them to be sectioned together to suit parties of any size. This shape is a signature of the design and reappears in the form of pink place mats and fuchsia 'Wavelength' sofas in the lounge. The use of organic shapes and bright colours really comes to fruition in the swimming pool, with a green, brown and blue mosaic decorating its base. The pool walls are otherwise white, forming curved steps up one side. Uncharacteristically, the surround features both wooden decking and sun-loungers – a rare use of natural materials and colours by a man who wishes to push the potential of manufacturing techniques.

Athens is so rooted in its ancient past that it is rarely associated with progressive architecture and design. Even the 2004 Olympics, which gave rise to a wash of new building projects (many of which, sadly, are already being labelled as white elephants), has done little to suggest that the city is on the cutting edge of contemporary culture. However, Greek classicism was originally a forward-thinking, innovative architectural adventure. Along with other Athenian newcomers such as the Fresh Hotel and Life Gallery, Rashid's Semiramis offers a radical enclave for those returning from the Parthenon.

Opposite: **Semiramis, Athens.** The base of the morphotic pool is decorated with a colourful mosaic. The right-hand side of the pool forms the lip of the decking area

Hotel Name	Semiramis
Address	48 Charilaou Trikoupi Street, 145 62 Kefalari – Kifissia, Athens, Greece
Telephone	+30 210 62 84 400 or design hotels™ 00800 37 46 83 57
Website	www.semiramisathens.com
Design style	Colourful plastic-fantastic
No. of rooms	42 rooms, 6 bungalows, 3 penthouse studios, 1 penthouse suite
Bars and restaurants	Connected bar (70 seats), restaurant (75 seats) and lounge (45 seats) areas
Spa facilities	Heated outdoor swimming pool. Mini gym, Jacuzzi, wellness programmes, beauty treatments, massage and personal trainer available
Clientele	Wealthy, international Karim Rashid junkies

Above: **Semiramis, Athens.** The lounge and restaurant features Rashid-designed 'Kab' chairs

Left: **Semiramis, Athens.** The bulbous ceiling hangs ominously above the lounge

Above: **Semiramis, Athens.** Balcony of the standard Semiramis room. The wall pattern is the same as that on the pink carpet in the lounge area

Above: **Semiramis, Athens.** The bathrooms of the Penthouse Suite and Studios have mirrored mosaic bath panels, translucent pink shower screens and green, cantilevered, box-shaped basins

Above: **Semiramis, Athens.** An opaque, curving glass wall sections off the bathroom in the standard rooms. The blue-glass washbasin has fittings by Dornbracht

Opposite: Semiramis, Athens. The Penthouse Suite has the hotel's trademark combination of white walls, translucent fittings and colourful furnishings, including a pink 'Swing' chair designed by Karim Rashid

Above: Semiramis, Athens. Green dominates the colour scheme of the Penthouse Suite bedroom. The balcony, topped with pink Plexiglas, looks out onto the Attica countryside

Above: **Semiramis, Athens.** One of the highlights of the Penthouse Suite is the veranda, with its terrazzo flooring and balcony topped with box-hedges

Opposite: **Semiramis, Athens.** Detail of the hotel's terrace

Q!
GRAFT

Location: **Berlin**
Completion date: **2004**

Q! emerged on the Berlin hotel and bar scene in 2004 with nowhere near as much fanfare as its radical design deserved. Perhaps this is because its fairly conservative exterior suggests little of the concept that literally unfolds beyond. However, it is now starting to win a clutch of awards including Best Hotel of the Year at the Leisure and Travel Design Awards 2005. In terms of innovation, its interior architecture knocks spots off city neighbours such as Ku'Damm 101 and rivals the best that Hamburg – the most progressive German city for new hotel design – has to offer.

GRAFT's concept is a cocoon of folds, waves, creases, loops and rounded corners, where much of the furniture is integrated into sweeps of material that rise up from the floor or out from the walls. Sharp corners and deadening planes are all but eradicated as the guest is enveloped into this protective world. Designer Thomas Willemeit says that the effect is to make 'guests change their interaction with furniture and architecture and become the actors on the lifestyle stage … it is as if the room has been formed by movement'. Indeed, in the standard rooms, which have an emphasis on slate, dark wood and white, the bed is set into a rolling wooden slope that curves up from the floor and goes on to form the bathroom area. The wooden side to the wardrobe curves out to become a flat shelf, while the ceiling has an inner skin that curves down the wall, disguising the marriage of horizontal and vertical planes. The skin is printed with indistinct female shapes that morph into one another: the colours and materials of the room designs are masculine, but they are presented as feminine forms. There is no barrier between the main room and washing area, which is differentiated by slate flooring. In the studios, a bathtub is sunk into the wooden slope that rises up from the bed. The power shower is housed in a large slate rectangle, with a clear glass door separating it from the rest of the room. Only the WC is isolated, for privacy's sake.

This sense of the free-flowing, hybridised space dominates the communal areas as well. The ground floor is wrapped in a red internal skin, made from Marmoleum, which folds to form furniture, levels and walls inside the external box. The reception desk rises up in a wave from the red floor, while the sharp angled wall behind, which curves over to create the ceiling, also forms a feature of the bar that lies behind it. The bar/restaurant, which is a private club available only to hotel guests and members, monopolises the ground floor. The bar-counter forms the axis in the centre of the space, dividing it casually into restaurant and lounge areas. The lounge is the most impressive result of GRAFT's wish to create a cocoon. The red lining unfolds in a seamless movement of walls, ceiling, gradations and seating. Lit white panels have been inserted into the angles where the waves have broken away from the main plane, while the bar frontage is a larger panel of white which provides the most obvious light source in the space. Apart from the integrated seating, there are low, geometrical divans, covered with grey suede.

The swooning curves and folds are all but dropped in

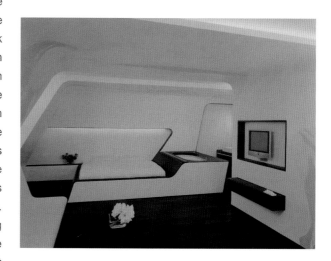

Above: **Q!, Berlin.** In the studios, the dark wood slopes up from the floor to create the bed level, and up again to house the bathtub. The design is seamless and conveys motion

Opposite: **Q!, Berlin.** The hotel's facade may not be particularly adventurous, but the reception area introduces the design concept of an inner skin that morphs from walls, floors and ceilings to create multi-levels and furniture. The reception desk rises as a wave out of the flooring while the wall slopes inwards and arcs over to form the ceiling

Hotel name	Q!
Address	Knesebeckstrasse 67, 10623 Berlin, Germany
Telephone	+49 (0)30 81 00 66 0
Website	www.q-berlin.de
Design style	Ultra-modern, cool, cornerless cocoon
No. of rooms	72 rooms, 4 studios, 1 penthouse
Bars and restaurants	Q! Die Bar, restaurant and bar for guests and members
Spa facilities	Sandraum, Japanese washing area, massages, solarium, Finnish sauna and yoga. Korres natural products
Clientele	Artistic, media and very design-savvy crowd

the basement spa, where the normal order of planes and tangents is restored. The materials, though, continue the wood and slate theme of the upstairs rooms. The treatment room has large, sliding wooden doors that lead into the Japanese washing area. This is tiled with slate on both the floor and wall, and has small wooden box seats and a low washing bench. The spa, which has the expected sauna and solarium, is subdued and peaceful, but it does have one unusual surprise. The Sandraum is a beguiling relaxation space which has orange loungers on a heated sand floor. The sand keeps the body at a stable temperature while the waft of aromatic oils fills the air.

GRAFT, famous for designing a Los Angeles studio and guesthouse for Brad Pitt, is in fact a hybrid in its own right, creating clubs, apartments, art installations, computer games and music from offices in Los Angeles, Berlin and Beijing. It doesn't seem to be confined by the linearity of a normal practice, and designs spaces and events that require us to project new interpretations in familiar settings.

Left: Q!, Berlin. The slate shower zone is integrated into the room. The vertical and horizontal planes of wall and ceiling are softened by a curving inner skin, faintly printed with entwined female forms

Left: Q!, Berlin. In the penthouse, the usual slate, wood and white scheme is broken up by the red seating, harking back to the vibrant red of the ground floor

Above: Q!, Berlin. In the bar, privacy and mystery are created by the gauze curtains, which are impermeable at night, across the hotel's front window. The warm feel of GRAFT's cocoon is helped by the fire in the front area's dark, almost cubist central feature

Right: Q!, Berlin. One section of the red flooring folds upwards to create inbuilt seating while another curves over to enclose the bar area. The bar, which splits the front space from the restaurant area, is fronted by a lit white panel, while softer, more discreet lighting also comes from the angle of wall and ceiling

Above: **Q!, Berlin.** One of the hotel's most unusual features is the Wellness Sandraum. Hot sand floors, heated loungers and aromatherapy oils are used to create an atmosphere of calm

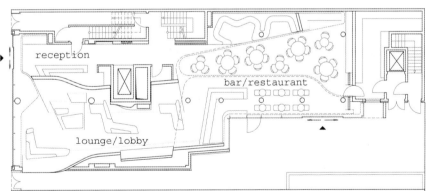

Opposite: **Q!, Berlin.** The spa has similar textures and hues to the guestrooms, but is a far more linear space. The Japanese washroom has low box stools

Above: **Q!, Berlin.** Ground-floor plan

Hotel on Rivington

Grzywinski Pons Architects/India Mahdavi/ Marcel Wanders/Piero Lissoni

Location: **New York**
Completion date: **2005**

Not surprisingly, the New York hotel scene has been lacklustre since the 9/11 attacks, especially in terms of innovative new architecture and design. Dream (a hotel) doesn't seem to have become the reality that everyone hoped for, while Gansevoort and the Maritime are pleasant enough, but hardly ground-breaking. It has been left to the Hotel on Rivington (sometimes known as THOR) to turn hopeful whispers into a radical reality. Even its conception was hit with some worrying pitfalls – it was originally going to be called the Surface Hotel, a physical embodiment of *Surface* magazine's dynamic design, but the latter's involvement ended during the development – and completion has taken four years. Fortunately, the project's leading designers stayed on board and the European-based trio of Marcel Wanders, India Mahdavi and Piero Lissoni form a line-up of some of the hottest design talent around.

The building is a 21-storey glass tower providing unobstructed views of the city. Designed by Matthew Grzywinski and Amador Pons, in collaboration with owner Paul Stallings, the facade features a pattern of tinted glass in an aluminium grid. Stallings is a property developer who has been influential in reinvigorating Manhattan's Lower East Side into a creative, youthful, stylish and cosmopolitan quarter since the late 1970s. Fittingly, the tower doubles up as the residence for his family of eight.

The 30-square-metre rooms, designed by India Mahdavi, are a third bigger than the New York average and are conceived to feel like apartments rather than hotel rooms. The design ensures that – from inside at least – the hotel is integrated into the Lower East Side scene, with rooms benefiting from floor-to-ceiling glazing and a private outdoor space. Even the shower walls form part of the facade – guests can make the utmost of the views while still being concealed from onlookers by a frosted panel. The bathrooms are large and form a significant part of the design's attempt to give the guest

a feeling of permanent apartment living rather than hotel transience. They feature two-person, Japanese-style tubs as well as the steam shower, and are decorated with luxurious Bisazza mosaic tiles. The furniture is modern, including comfortable, cubic armchairs and Tempur-Pedic mattresses. The rooms are colour-themed, from dark hues to fresh lemon, with the armchairs and carpets matching the tiles that cover both the walls and floor of the bathroom. Mod cons include heated floors in the bathrooms, flat-screen televisions set into the walls, on-demand entertainment and programmable, motorised curtains, but the real coup of Hotel on Rivington remains the combination of clear and frosted glazing.

Down below, Dutch designer Marcel Wanders' 'Eggtrance' entranceway is a shock. A blood-red pathway runs between his snowflake Bisazza mosaic walls and spills into a Gaudí-esque, sculptural ice grotto

Above: **Hotel on Rivington, New York.** Marcel Wanders' 'Eggtrance' to the hotel features his snowflake design in Bisazza mosaic and an ice-like grotto created from structured foam

Opposite: **Hotel on Rivington, New York.** The 21-storey glass facade towers over the mostly low-rise Lower East Side of Manhattan

Hotel name	Hotel on Rivington
Address	107 Rivington Street, New York, NY 10002, USA
Telephone	+1 212 475 2600
Website	www.hotelonrivington.com
Design style	Shining glass tower with clean, contemporary interiors and touches of Marcel Wanders-lust
No. of rooms	91 rooms, 19 suites
Bars and restaurants	100-seater restaurant & bar
Spa facilities	In-room spa amenities and services by Paul LaBrecque
Clientele	Music- and media-mad creatives drawn to the Lower East Side scene. It's Moby's favourite hotel

(created from foam coated with fibreglass-reinforced concrete). It is like being inside a giant version of Wanders' infamous Egg Vase design, whose shape was created by stuffing hard-boiled eggs into a latex rubber condom. The red theme also shoots up the heart of the hotel in the form of red-leather-lined elevators. Wanders has also designed the ground-floor, skylit restaurant and bar, while Piero Lissoni has created the second-floor lobby, lined with ebony wood and lit by a Venini chandelier, which is a private reception area for hotel guests only. This is the first American venture for Lissoni,

whose acclaimed work includes the refurbishment of the Hotel Monaco & Grand Canal in Venice.

The Surface Penthouse, a 230-square-metre triplex, affords three-sided views of New York and includes a 90-square-metre exterior deck. It was originally to be designed by Zaha Hadid, but ultimately Grzywinski Pons Architects themselves created the interior. The views are so incredible because the Hotel on Rivington looms high above the other buildings of the Lower East Side, which is predominantly made up of 19th-century, low-rise, brickwork buildings. The district is becoming a focal point for new restaurants and bars, but until now has offered little in the way of hotel accommodation. Even though there are few major tourist sites in the area, the hotel should prove a draw for the creative travellers whose home-grown equivalents have revitalised the area. The owners of 60 Thompson, one of the hippest hotels in New York, are now planning their own venture nearby.

Left and below: Hotel on Rivington, New York.
Some of India Mahdavi's guestroom interiors, featuring comfortable armchairs and a furry pouf, have a dark-themed design which is carried through to the Bisazza-tiled bathroom

Right: Hotel on Rivington, New York. The private guests' lobby, designed by Italian Piero Lissoni, combines dark ebony wood and light-coloured furnishings

Below: Hotel on Rivington, New York. The bathrooms feature tiling on the floor and walls, and include a two-person, Japanese-style bath

Above and below: **Hotel on Rivington, New York.**
It's all about the view at the Hotel on Rivington,
which makes the most of the building's height with
floor-to-ceiling glazing

Left: **Hotel on Rivington, New York.** A yellow-
themed guestroom, featuring a Tempur-Pedic bed
and silver coffee table. Mahdavi, who is Iranian-born
but based in Paris, has also designed interiors for
the Townhouse in Miami and the Condesa df in
Mexico City

Omm

Juli Capella/Sandra Tarruella & Isabel López Vilalta

Location: **Barcelona**
Completion date: **2004**

Opening a designer hotel in the centre of one of Europe's great cities of style raises expectations but Grupo Tragaluz's Omm, near the popular shopping street Passeig de Gràcia in Barcelona's Eixample district, delivers with an intriguing exterior. From certain angles, the building appears to be windowless. Sections of the Cabra limestone peel away from the facade, like the half-opened doors of an advent calendar, and curve out towards the street. Behind these curves lie the hotel's balconies and windows which can barely be seen even from directly across the street. The result is that the front rooms have a private balcony even though they face onto a busy road, and also capture the optimum amount of sunshine. The rooms to the rear also feature balconies, protected by a horizontal metal grille that is dressed with hanging vegetation. Omm's rooms are relatively compact, so the architectural solution has been to incorporate a private relationship with the outside world on both facades.

Above the red reception desk are three illuminated 'M's, reflecting the name of the hotel and its Moo and Moovida restaurant spaces. Further in, the interior benefits from Grupo Tragaluz's experience of running successful, stylish but quite informal restaurants. The group's own interior designers, Sandra Tarruella and Isabel López Vilalta have created comfortable but elegant communal spaces which appeal to local Barceloneses as well as the guests. Visible through the exterior glazing, the grey lobby lounge is an inviting space rather than a thoroughfare. Seating includes high-cushioned Perobell sofas and Jacobsen 'Egg' chairs while a fireplace, set within a section cut through an internal wall, adds to the feeling of permanency. The lobby's double height is augmented by two huge, pink 'Oven' lamps by Antoni Arola.

Lighting has been well thought-through on the ground floor, which features nine electronically adjustable, cuboid skylights bringing natural light into the Moo and Moovida restaurants and bar. Attached to the bar space, Moovida is based around a central, communal table with 'LEM' bar stools and sets the black-and-white theme of the main restaurant which is

visible through a screen of fine metal mesh. Moo offers experimental Catalan dishes and is overseen by the Roca brothers, whose Celler de Can Roca in Gironda has two Michelin stars. Diners sit on black or bleached 'Kayak' chairs designed by Jorge Pensi. Perhaps the best area of Moo is by the white interior courtyard which houses a bamboo garden along with wall-mounted black, white and silver shields that divert light into the restaurant. Below ground lies Ommsession, a club and event space with cubic chairs and soft, colourful 'beanbag' tables that support metal trays.

Upstairs the rooms are reached through a deliberately dark, oppressive corridor which creates a contrast with the light, airy rooms which are uncluttered and decorated

Above: **Omm, Barcelona.** The hall lobby is an inviting social space that can be seen through the glazed ground-floor facade. Dark colours and 'Loft' sofas, designed by Lluís Codina for Perobell, ensure that this seems to be a less transitory hotel lobby

Opposite: **Omm, Barcelona.** Above the glazed ground floor, sections of the hotel's facade peel away to reveal windows and balconies. Effectively, they are limestone-clad shutters that provide privacy, can be adjusted according the position of the sun, and create a very distinctive architectural feature

Hotel name	Omm
Address	Rosselló 265, Barcelona 08008, Spain
Telephone	+34 934 454 000 or design hotels™ 00800 37 46 83 57
Website	www.hotelomm.es
Design style	Contemporary cool behind an ultra-modern advent calendar
No. of rooms	58 rooms, 1 suite
Bars and restaurants	Bar; Moo and Moovida restaurants; Ommsession club
Spa facilities	O2 Spa to open in late 2005
Clientele	Young and urban. Facilities popular with local Barcelonese

with a combination of white and natural colours. Signature furniture items include bleached 'Kayak' chairs once more (but here in the single-stem, swivel version) upon light, wooden floorboards. The bedroom is partitioned from the bathroom by a glossy white wall that features an inset, flat-screen television. The bathroom itself looks out onto the street, benefiting from the privacy afforded by the licks of limestone.

One of Omm's major attractions is the roof terrace and bar, which is only available to guests. The mix of metal grille and vegetation that decorates the rear facade is used again here to dress the all-wooden decking that steps up to an open-air pool. Antonio Gaudí's Casa Milá can be viewed from white 'Luna' sun-loungers and Philippe Starck 'Bubble Club' chairs. Omm is at its best when it forms a connection with its Barcelona surroundings.

Above right: **Omm, Barcelona.** Nine skylights pierce Moo's ceiling to bring natural light into the restaurant, which serves adventurous Catalan dishes. Furniture includes Jorge Pensi's 'Kayak' chairs, manufactured by Sare

Above: **Omm, Barcelona.** The exterior, limestone curls are optimised to allow a great deal of light into the bedrooms while affording privacy from passers-by below. All the rooms are square, with a white partition sectioning off the bathroom

Above: **Omm, Barcelona.** Unlike the exterior features, the room design is not particularly experimental. Pale furniture and fittings include bleached, swivel versions of the 'Kayak' chairs

Right: **Omm, Barcelona.** The dark corridors create a deliberate contrast with the light rooms

Above: **Omm, Barcelona.** Below-ground, the Ommsession club has 'soft' tables that support metal trays

Below: **Omm, Barcelona.** The hotel design is at its best when it interacts with the city. The roof terrace, with wooden decking and Starck-designed chairs, offers excellent views of Barcelona

Below: **Omm, Barcelona.** The rooms have wall-mounted music systems and internet connectivity

micro
budget

Architecturally, the major cities of the world are a breeding ground for problems and restraints, but also for creative responses. Tokyo, New York and London have outgrown themselves, which leads to an inward compression of space and, of course, places a premium on land.

Tokyo has consistently dealt with the problem in innovative ways. Making the most out of limited space is part of the essence of the city's cultural character. Creative responses have long been vital: apartments are smaller, but they are aided by the benefits of technology. The ultimate progress in the utility of space and a response to metropolitan life is the capsule hotel. Originally aimed at the businessman who has worked too long hours – or got too drunk – to go home, they were established in the 1970s and are centred on the Shibuya district. Some Westerners regard their design as inhumane, and they certainly are not designed with claustrophobics in mind. Usually, the hotels are made up of coffin-sized boxes stacked on top of each other, with each capsule containing little more than some bedding. Consequently, it is possible to house 16 to 20 capsules in the space that would serve as one double room in a normal Western-style hotel. City compression has also increased the popularity of 'love hotels', which are usually quite small but often done up as kitschy as possible, with revolving beds and vibrating chairs. They have been around in one form or another since the Edo period and are not just used for prostitution. They are popular with the young who cannot afford their own apartments or, if they can, are fed up with the plywood walls that allow all the neighbours to hear rather too much. With a straightforwardness which is so foreign to Western sensibilities, the hotels offer hourly 'rests' to couples.

micro budget

Above: **25hours, Hamburg.** The budget hotel makes the most of its space with multi-purpose rooms and functional furnishings, combined with touches of luxury

It has taken Western hotel culture a long time to absorb the Japanese response to inner-city compression, but the change is coming. This has been spurred on by the intensification of travel, boosted by the emergence of no-frills, cheap airlines. Between 1992 and 2002, the number of passengers flying to or from Britain rose from 82 million to 146 million, and it is continuing to rise. Flight has become more democratic than ever, but many European cities have a distinct lack of good-quality, low-budget accommodation to meet the demand. YOtel and easyHotel are leading the way, taking the idea of the capsule hotel to create windowless pods so space can be utilised to the utmost. However, rather than capsules, the pods are small en-suite rooms, where an innovative design ethos, borrowed from aircraft and ship cabin design, is combined with high technology to create surprisingly exciting environments. Interestingly, YOtel and easyHotel are cross-branded from other industries – conveyor-belt sushi bars and budget airline respectively. Other players are likely to include the owners of the Pret a Manger sandwich chain which now monopolises London's streets. The hotel market is being shaken up by newcomers who are using the wisdom gained in other businesses to revolutionise expectations. More experienced hoteliers, such as André Balazs in the United States and Ken McCulloch in Britain, are also reacting to the explosion of design literacy by shaking up the traditional, functional and loveless business and budget markets with low-cost, high-design concepts. The quality of design and service at the Dakota, McCulloch's motorway hotel near Nottingham, makes the bland offerings of the budget-business genre's established players seem totally unacceptable.

One American company, MetroNaps, has managed to outdo the Japanese in taking the functionalism of 'rest' accommodation to its most extreme border. Like the Tokyo innovations, it is a direct response to the problems of the metropolitan lifestyle but MetroNaps is not a hotel. Combining the capsule hotel's idea of an encased bed and the love hotel's concept of the very short-term lease, MetroNaps offers 20-minute powernaps to New York executives in an ergonomically designed, relaxation-inducing, reclining pod. Like some love hotels, it even features a vibrating chair, but the idea is to gently awaken you at the end of your session, rather than arouse you at the start.

YOtel

Priestman Goode

Location: **prototype**
Completion date: **2004**

It has taken a long time for other over-populated countries to adopt the Japanese capsule hotel concept. When it does finally arrive, though, it will bear little similarity to the stacked-up boxes that still service the needs of Japanese businessmen and adventurous tourists who are on an overnight stay. Rather, it will take the form of YOtel's 10.5-metre-square rooms that should appeal to the design-minded rather than the purely utilitarian. Taking elements of the capsule concept alongside advances made in first-class aircraft cabins, where a high level of comfort and wide range of amenities are found within a compact area, YOtel will attempt to offer modern concepts of luxury at an affordable price. YOtel chairman Simon Woodroffe is no stranger to introducing Japanese culture to the European market, having found great success offering low-priced, conveyor-belt Japanese food to Londoners through the YO! Sushi chain since 1997. YO! Sushi, which now has 20 outlets and is expanding overseas, placed an early marker for the popularity of sushi in Britain and brought with it other innovations such as the self-dispensing, counter-top drink taps.

The YOtel prototype is designed by Priestman Goode, who used their experience working on new Airbus double-decker aircrafts and Virgin trains to develop the hotel concept over a three-year period. The objective was to find solutions that would enable four- to five-star luxury to be costed at around £75 per night. Working within such a small room size, the use of space

is optimum. The design features a rotating double bed that doubles as a sofa, thereby enabling a greater amount of free space prior to bedtime. The 'techno wall' ensures that the very latest gadgetry is provided while using minimal space, and includes a wall-mounted, Sony flat-screen television, MP3, wireless internet access, surround-sound speaker system and a fold-down desk. In effect, the only luxury that YOtel will be missing is space, but claustrophobia is reduced by the use of light-coloured materials throughout the design. Technology will also lend itself to check-in facilities and room keys. Like many airlines, check-in/checkout will be electronic, thereby reducing staff overheads, while the key will be replaced by an electronic fingerprint sensor, developed by Mayhem UK Ltd.

Right: YOtel, prototype. The beech veneer on the walls prevents the light-coloured space becoming too sanitised. Next to the recessed hanging space, which replaces the traditional wardrobe, lies the 'techno wall'. A flat-screen television is set into the wall above a foldaway desk which also features access points for the latest technology

Opposite: YOtel, prototype. Capsule hotels and aeroplane cabins merge to form a design that also owes something to the cruise liner. Where possible, all elements are hidden or recessed, giving the design a touch of Art Deco linearity. Innovations include fingerprint entry and windows that look onto the corridor, rather than externally

Hotel name	YOtel
Address	Prototype
Website	www.yotel.co.uk
Design style	Spaceship cabin
Clientele	Stylish but skint interstellar sleep-seekers

Perhaps the greatest innovation for YOtel will be the way that it increases the number of 10-metre-square units within a shell by having internal rather than external windows. The windows will look onto the corridor, rather than forming part of the facade. This may seem off-putting, but rather than the only external light being created by a 24-hour neon blaze, the corridors will be naturally lit by a sophisticated combination of channelling and reflective mechanisms. YOtel believes that this will also help it place hotels in locations that would not usually be appropriate, reducing costs so that luxury can be bought at an affordable price.

Gerard Greene, YOtel's Chief Executive, says, 'It is not enough that a hotel is designed well, people want to be excited when they stay at a hotel.' YOtel responds to some of the lifestyle concepts that led to the boom in the boutique hotel genre – the increased public awareness of design, the individual's greater demand for an invigorating environment – but plans to deliver an affordable solution with a genuinely innovative design. Interestingly, whereas high-concept design has made boutique hotels expensive, YO! plans to use it to make hotels cheap. YO!'s established association with low-budget design sophistication may mean that it can start to roll out new hotels as quickly as nigiri on one of its smooth-running conveyor belts.

Above, left: YOtel, prototype. Glazing and mirrors are used to optimise light and space. Wherever possible, external elements such as shower controls and shelving are shallow or recessed

Above: YOtel, prototype. The rotating double bed
folds away to form a sofa. The en-suite bathroom,
featuring elements supplied by CP Hart, DuPont
Corian and Hansgrohe, is sectioned off from the
main area by glazing and, being watertight, can be
used as a wet room

easyHotel

EPR

Location: **London**
Completion date: **2005**

easyGroup has proved to be one of the greatest cross-branding successes in the modern era, quickly establishing a healthy market share in a range of services from cheap flights and car rental to internet cafés. The word 'easy' and the Group's brash, orange corporate identity has come to mean a cheap, no-frills service that, it seems, can be lent to almost any sector of industry. Only Virgin can rival its dexterity, but Richard Branson's multi-headed beast tends to focus on presenting mid-market products. The ethos of easyGroup is that anyone can afford its services, and it has played a huge part in the rapid democratisation of European travel through easyJet, offering seats at a previously unimaginable low price. Depending on availability, you can fly to London and hire a car for little more than the change in your pocket. With hindsight, it is obvious that the low-budget easyHotel brand was on the agenda. However, taking into account exorbitant London property prices, high rents and heart-attack-inducing hotel start-up costs, the main problem would be how on earth it could afford to offer a central London hotel room at the price 'easy' customers are prepared to pay. Stelios Haji-Ioannou, the chairman and founder of easyGroup, is known as a fearless financial miracle-worker, but surely this would be one 'water-into-wine' trick that couldn't come off.

Indeed, at first it seemed that the idea was doomed. Originally, the project was called easyDorm, but the decision was taken to up the ante and offer double rooms with en-suite services. Even at the budget end of the market, the London price for this is typically around £100 per night. easyHotel proposed a starting price for very early bookers of just … £5. As with most easyGroup products, the price increases with scarcity, but even the last available rooms are not expected to cost more than £70 per night at high season. The Group purchased a former hotel in the famously posh central London area of Kensington in May 2004, but the early design solutions were quoted at about £40,000 per room, which would have made the project financially untenable. The high costs were largely the result of attempting to provide bespoke designs for the en-suite rooms in a limited space (approximately five to seven square metres) while emphasising the easyHotel brand. Fortunately, EPR, whose hotel clients have included Marriott, Hilton and Le Meridien, stepped in to reinterpret the early prototypes with a seemingly simple solution that would only cost around 10 per cent of the original estimates. Every element of the room design is off-the-shelf, but it is impossible to tell, as EPR has created a unique, seamless pod branded with the unmistakable 'easy' orange colour.

All the components are prefabricated and slotted together on site. While YOtel has successfully absorbed the innovations of aeroplane cabin design, EPR looked to marine berths, appropriating the same space-saving wall partitions that were already being used in ship design and had been used for easyCruise, the Group's latest venture. The shell of the room is made from lightweight, coated metal, thereby increasing room space while still enabling enough soundproofing. The en-suite shower, toilet and basin are contained in prefabricated, watertight pods which are simply incorporated into the overall

Left and opposite: **easyHotel, London.** Some of the rooms are windowless, enabling greater use of the floorspace. easyGroup's distinctive orange branding has been leavened by white; easyCruise ship cabins had been criticised as 'too orange' for comfort

Hotel name	easyHotel
Address	14 Lexham Gardens, London W8 5JE, UK
Telephone	Online booking only
Website	www.easyhotel.com
Design style	Minimalist orange
No. of rooms	35 rooms
Bars and restaurants	None
Spa facilities	None
Clientele	Youth in search of cheap and cheerful solutions

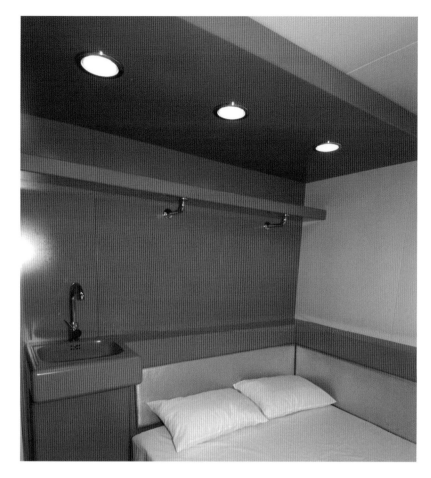

Above: **easyHotel, London.** The first easyHotel has 35 rooms, housed in a former 18-room hotel building in Kensington

Left and below: **easyHotel, London.** In the prototype design, which included largely bespoke, expensive elements, the placement of the basin was unresolved, standing within the main room. The finished design includes all bathroom facilities within a curved, pre-fabricated pod

design, while space issues were further helped by sourcing the smallest double mattresses that were already available. This removed the need for expensive foldaway solutions. Furthermore, easyHotel rooms have no windows, maximising the use of space to the extent that the former 18-room hotel now houses 35 rooms.

EPR have proven to be as deft as Stelios in getting

value for money. easyHotel are able to offer the £5 starting price, while breaking even at just £30 per room. The easyHotel room is not luxurious: it is purely a double bed with en-suite facilities, but it is a striking, functional design that allows the possibility of a prime location at minimal cost. Part of the beauty of EPR's solution is that the room design is so simple and flexible that future franchises will be able to use a manual to create an easyHotel with little reference to architects and designers. The company has already adapted the design for three room sizes (honestly called 'tiny', 'very small', and 'small') to suit the constraints of the Kensington building. The structure was not ideally suited for the first easyHotel, but Phil Waterson, the Senior Designer at EPR, says, 'That was actually quite fortunate because we know that making it work there will mean that we can make it work almost anywhere in the future.' As the easyHotel brand expands, franchisees will have to take into account local room-size regulations, but the manual already provides information about the adaptation of the model. There seems to be no doubt that orange pods will be springing up across Europe in the near future.

Above: **easyHotel, London.** It may be cheap and startlingly branded, but the easyHotel is not devoid of all modern luxuries

Above: **easyHotel, London.** Axonometric drawing of the floor layout

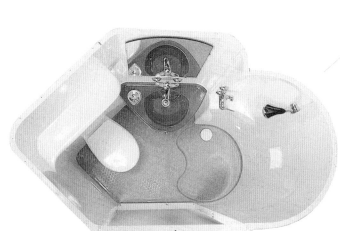

Left: **easyHotel, London.** The easyHotel branded, en-suite pod. All elements are pre-fabricated, so the wet-room style capsule is merely plumbed in on-site

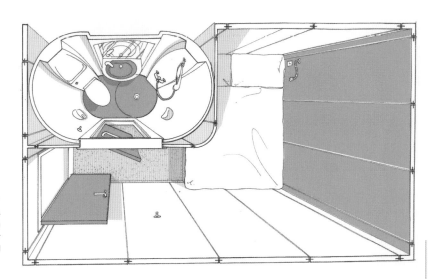

Right: **easyHotel, London.** Sketch of the 'tiny' room design, showing how the en-suite pod is placed within the compact room. 'Small' and 'very small' rooms have space at the side or end of the bed

MetroNaps

MetroNaps

Location: **New York**
Completion date: **2004**

Much of new hotel design seems to be born out of usually quite referential visions of the future, but MetroNaps is the future: it is the endgame of hotel functionalism. MetroNaps takes the original purpose of the hotel – to provide sleeping accommodation in a location away from home – and pushes it to a radical, pared-down but hyper-technological extreme that must impress even the Japanese. The capsule hotels reduced the facility of the hotel down to tubular pods, the size of a slim single bed, that are stacked on top of each other. Location is the prime luxury. The same is true of MetroNaps, which, like the capsule hotels, is a reaction to the metropolitan lifestyle and scarcity of city-space. However, MetroNaps is not designed for anything as leisurely as a night-time kip: it is designed for 20-minute powernaps.

The pods are placed in prime locations so that city-workers can continue to perform at their optimum during long, stressful days. MetroNaps wears its scientific credentials on its sleeve. Designed to maximise the rejuvenating potential of a brief rest, it was researched and tested at Carnegie Mellon University as a professional, scientific alternative to the powernap or desk-doze, which is usually done in such an awkward environment that the benefit is much reduced. Harvard Medical School research has shown that a midday nap may protect the brain circuits from overuse so that they can absorb more information and heighten skills: consequently people will be more productive throughout a working day if they sleep briefly during it. Part of MetroNaps' beauty is that they are stand-alone units that can be put in any office space: at 120 centimetres high, 120 centimetres wide and 200 centimetres long, all they require is less than two square metres and a power supply. Weighing only 131 kilograms, with four attachable wheels, they are also portable. Consequently, the facility can extend itself to any location – such as airports, train stations or convention centres – that are a focal point for the time-poor. One can even imagine them within high-class shopping centres, so that fashion junkies can have a powernap to give them the energy to extend their power-shop. The look of the MetroNaps

pods may also appeal to them: the original idea may have been crisply functional, but the design is quite exciting and enticing in a way that even the best capsule design has never managed (the latter seem doomed to conjure up images of coffins and tinned sardines).

The first MetroNaps location is within the Empire State Building, where they form rows of white orbs beneath circular wall-lights – it looks as though an alien-hatching station has been placed in the heart of one the United States' great architectural symbols. The tired-out workers make their way to Suite 2410 and pay $13.45 (or less, if they're serial nappers) for a 20-minute snooze which will refresh them for the rest of the day. At their simplest, the pods are comfortable, contoured loungers, with a gel-coated fibreglass orb forming a protective enclave around the head and upper body. A tinted visor can also be drawn down to further induce the feeling of a cocoon. The pod can be reclined at various angles for

Above: MetroNaps, New York. The original MetroNaps opened on the 24th floor of the Empire State Building in May 2004. The customer cannot see the other pods, giving them the feeling of a solitary cocoon

Opposite: MetroNaps, New York. The pod shells are made from lightweight, gel-coated fibreglass and are fixed onto a powder-coated steel tray

Hotel name	MetroNaps
Address	Empire State Building, 350 Fifth Avenue, New York, NY 10118, USA
Telephone	+1 212 239 3344
Website	www.metronaps.com
Design style	Space-age pods
No. of rooms	8 pods
Bars and restaurants	Food can be ordered
Spa facilities	None
Clientele	Time-poor businesspeople looking for rapid solutions

maximum comfort, with the feet and knees raised to increase blood circulation and reduce pressure on the lower back. The customer drifts off listening to tranquil, sleep-inducing music through Bose QuietComfort 2 Noise Cancelling headphones. At the end of the session, they are gently awoken through a combination of light change and vibration that is set by a programmable 'logic-controller'. Lotions, facial spritz and lemon-scented hand-towels are available for a final dose of refreshment before the worker bee faces the city's hurly-burly once more.

MetroNaps is only likely to appeal to those who are motivated by a hectic game of optimum achievement. Much of modern hotel culture has arisen as an antidote to time-consciousness and hamster-on-a-wheel processes, while MetroNaps actually enables greater corporatism and productivity. Yet MetroNaps provides the same facility as many luxury hotels – it is a retreat from the city, if only for 20 minutes. Its purpose also synchronises with the original, elemental luxury that lies at the heart of hotel culture: the need for a bed in the right place at the right time.

Right: MetroNaps, New York. The MetroNaps lounger-pod, with the tinted visor lowered. The customer purchases a 20-minute pass, adjusts the pod settings, puts on soundproof headphones and takes a powernap

Below: MetroNaps, New York. Customers are gently awoken by a subtle change in the light and vibrations from the chair-back

Above: MetroNaps, Vancouver. There is a second MetroNaps site at Vancouver International Airport, providing a nap facility for pilots and airport staff, as well as passengers

Left: MetroNaps, New York. Ergonomically designed, the pods incline forward for initial entry and recline to suit individual comfort

Dakota

Amanda Rosa

Location: **Nottingham**
Completion date: **2004**

Ken McCulloch (the originator of the successful Malmaison hotel chain), Formula 1 racing driver David Coulthard and property developer Peter Morris have entered the budget market with a new concept, the Dakota, which they hope will spawn offspring all over the United Kingdom. As detailed in this Micro Budget section, new budget hotel culture is borrowing solutions from aeroplane technology and design, so it is fitting that this new chain is named after a plane. With an elegant combination of style and functionalism, the Douglas DC-3 'Dakota' helped to expand the possibility of air travel for Average Joes following its maiden flight in 1935. (DC is also the nickname of David Coulthard, so the Dakota name may be a private joke between the owners.) The

Above: **Dakota, Nottingham.** The high-ceilinged lobby, with comfortable leather seating and an open fireplace, bucks the business-budget trend for small, sterile receptions

Opposite: **Dakota, Nottingham.** The black granite and glass exterior is stylish but foreboding

link to flight is taken further, with huge images of the plane used strikingly within the interior, and a promotional tagline of 'Travel Business Class, pay Economy'. The first location, in Nottingham's Sherwood Business Park off the M1 motorway's Junction 27, may seem a rather uninspiring place for a launch and hardly evokes the razzmatazz of the F1 circuit. However, the hoteliers' ambition is to offer good design, at low prices, in the right place for business customers. The Nottingham setting may also attract some tourists, but the Dakota is aimed at disgruntled business customers who are bored by the anonymity, low design and invisible service of mid- to low-price chains.

The Dakota announces itself with a hulking, somewhat ominous, black granite exterior. It is assertive, confident and quite unlike usual hotel architecture, suggesting a high-tech industry headquarters rather than a roadside waystation. The tall reception lobby, with oversized furniture, a large, open fireplace below an inset bookcase, and images of the Dakota aeroplane, is the antithesis of past budget-hotel design, where the reception is regarded as a waste of space and consequently small and uncomfortable. Throughout the social spaces, the austerity of the exterior has been replaced by a friendlier, more comfortable atmosphere, combining hardwood floors, reclaimed brickwork, leather furniture and exposed air-conditioning ducts in a way that is reminiscent of a loft apartment or warehouse conversion. Unusually for a business hotel, the Dakota is a social haven, with a decent-sized grill restaurant and bar.

The interiors are by Amanda Rosa, McCulloch's partner, who created the look of the early Malmaisons (McCulloch has now sold the chain) and his more recent venture, the Columbus chain. She has carried the warm simplicity of the social areas, and the combination of brickwork, leather and wood, through to the bedrooms. They are 25 square metres and feel reasonably sized, partly due to the number of items of furniture being kept to a minimum. However, there is no meanness to the proportions of the standard components: the beds are large, the plasma-screen television is 32-inch and there's

Hotel name	Dakota
Address	Lakeview Drive, Sherwood Business Park, Nottingham NG15 0DA, UK
Telephone	+44 (0)870 442 2727
Website	www.dakotahotels.co.uk
Design style	Manhattan loft inside a sci-fi box
No. of rooms	92 rooms
Bars and restaurants	Bar and grill restaurant
Spa facilities	Fitness room
Clientele	Mostly business travellers and the odd Robin Hood enthusiast

a walk-through shower. As is essential for the modern business hotel, the design also incorporates a work station with broadband access. Space has been saved through under-bed drawers, while a suit-hanging area is hidden craftily within the open-ended panelling behind the bed. The use of dark wood, silver chrome bed lights, black-and-white bathroom tiles and a framed box around the television add luxurious or interesting touches that aren't usually expected of budget hotel design.

Some years ago, Coulthard was subjected to plane-orientated misfortune with his involvement, as a passenger, in a terrible accident. However, the early signs are that the new Dakota seems to be a secure investment that is well prepared for the long haul. Grand plans are already drawn up for business-friendly locations near motorways, airports, business parks and city centres – it will be interesting to see whether the low price and room size can be replicated for suitable inner-city sites. The quality of design at Dakota seems to have surprised everybody. *Condé Nast Traveler* has put the hotel in its 2005 'Hot List' and the UK national press has been queuing up to praise it. Old hands at the business chain trade are quickly assembling plans to counter with

upgrades in comfort and design. Despite its associations with anonymous functionalism, it seems that the business sector of hotel design will be revolutionised more quickly by the 'high-design, low-cost' mantra than the tourist genre.

Above and below: Dakota, Nottingham. The bar and grill areas are separated by a wooden screen. A combination of wood, leather and exposed brickwork is used throughout the interior

Left and below: **Dakota, Nottingham.** The rooms have a large amount of wood panelling. This is used to hide the open hanging space behind the bed

25hours

3Meta

Location: **Hamburg**
Completion date: **2003**

The very name 25hours suggests that there's more to life than you would normally expect. This is certainly true of the hotel's design, which offers an aesthetic experience well beyond the level suggested by its budget room rate (59 euros for under-25s). That is not to say that 25hours is luxurious: guests expecting quality amenities and expensive materials would be disappointed. However, designers 3Meta (made up of interior designer, Evi Märklstetter and designer, Armin Fischer) have met the challenge of balancing maximum utility and style through a democratic approach to interior design.

The building was originally a storage hall which local firm HPV extended outwards, with the addition of two

Above: 25hours, Hamburg. The hotel's style is based on affordable design. The curving reception desk, clad with convex mirrored disks, sits on a shock of pink

Opposite: 25hours, Hamburg. The five-storey building was converted from a 1950s storage hall, with the addition of two floors and new wings

storeys to allow the hotel to house 65 rooms. The facade is not particularly noticeable or extravagant, but inside, the reception declares that the hotel wishes to invigorate the mind and appeal to the design-savvy media-types visiting this area of Hamburg. The circular reception desk sits upon a furry pink Kasthall rug, and is clad with 420 mirrored baubles. Beyond, the space for facilities is limited, forcing the designers to push the boundaries of that base principle of so much hotel design: multi-use.

The Tageswandel bar is an extreme example of how to extract many functions and moods from the same area. Naturally, it also serves as the restaurant. The white, U-shaped, Corian bar-counter stands in front of an open kitchen and protrudes into the centre of the room. As the 'day bar', the space provides a self-service setting for breakfast, and then becomes a snack bar, before turning into a sushi restaurant. Apart from the white bar stools, further seating is provided by beige sofas and white armchairs towards the lounge area. Later on, the kitchen is screened by a curtain and the 'night bar' takes over, with bar staff and DJs taking up residence. Lighting is key to creating the moods that match this multi-use, with an integrated light-rail helping change the space from bright-white morning café to sultry nightspot.

25hours' other communal areas are similarly multi-functional. The lobby flows into the 'event lounge', a large, 320-square-metre space that can act as the hotel lounge or can be divided into three 'Freiraum' (Free Room) areas to meet the particular needs of events and launches. The lounge has a glass-enclosed fire in the centre and, for normal hotel use, grey Living Divani sofas, red stools and white cubes, along with c-shaped white metal tables. Upstairs on the third floor, residents have access to the 24-hour Living Room where they can lounge, watch films, play table football, or use the six-metre-long zebrano-wood table. This table is lit from above by striking, coloured Perspex domes. The 24-hour facility is made possible by removing the need for staff as all food and drink is self-service from vending machines.

This paring down of services stretches to the bedrooms. There's no minibar or toiletries so the guest

Hotel name	25hours
Address	Paul-Dessau-Straße 2, 22761 Hamburg, Germany
Telephone	+49 (0)40 855 07 0 or design hotels™ 00800 37 46 83 57
Website	www.25hours-hotel.com
Design style	1960s retro brings high design to light pockets
No. of rooms	89 rooms
Bars and restaurants	Bar Tageswandel serves breakfast, snacks and sushi at various times of the day
Spa facilities	None
Clientele	Young media-workers too design-savvy for hostels

must purchase anything they require from the reception. Cheekily, this is described as a bonus as it promotes interaction and 'communication', which is a main ethos behind the design of the communal areas. Despite this slightly disingenuous sleight of hand, the hotel rooms are genuinely spurred on by principles of interaction and democracy. 3Meta's purpose-designed fittings include a multi-functional MDF desk that veers down to become a seat or luggage rack. On either side, the plinth of the bed base reaches out to form a space that can be used as a bedside table or shelving. In the bathroom area, the washbasin surround folds under to provide under-sink storage. These all-white features are not glamorous, but they are beautifully functional. Almost all the furniture and accessories, including Sebastian Wrong's 'Spun 1' table lamp, manufactured by Flos, can be purchased from the reception. The 'Parentesi' bedside lamps, also by Flos, can be run up or down vertical cables to alter lighting as required.

25hours has a fluidity that is meant to appeal to its core audience of young trendsetters. It responds to their lifestyle with a lack of spatial and temporal restrictions and a keen eye on the immediacy of modern consumerism.

Above: 25hours, Hamburg. Seen here in its 'Day' persona, the bar is dominated by a Corian counter. Lighting is used to carry the venue through a multiplicity of functions from breakfast bar to nightspot

Left: 25hours, Hamburg. Movable mirrors form a wall that curves from the lobby area towards the lift

Right: 25hours, Hamburg. There is a simple, retro feel to both the communal areas and the rooms

Above: **25hours, Hamburg.** The bathroom is integrated into the main space, with the exception of the toilet behind a sliding door. The basin-surround folds under to provide towel storage

Above: **25hours, Hamburg.** TThe desk surface falls down to form a lower level that can be used as a luggage rack or seat. Almost all items that are used in the design, including the 'Spun 1' table lamp, can be bought in the reception

Right: **25hours, Hamburg.** The residents' multipurpose 24-hour Living Room has a six-metre-long zebrano-wood table

QT HotelsAB/ROY

Location: **New York**
Completion date: **2005**

South African architect Lindy Roy, head of New York-based ROY, has designed some extremely radical hotel concepts including the Okavango Delta Spa, involving a range of free-floating and fixed structures in the Botswana swampland, and Wind River Lodge, an extreme heli-ski hotel in Alaska. Either of these projects would merit a place in any compendium of revolutionary hotel design. Unfortunately, as happens with so many younger architects, few of her designs have been realised, with projects plagued with delays or cancellations that are beyond her control. However, 2003 saw the opening of her first permanent structure, the Vitra design showroom in New York's meat-packing district, right next door to Soho House. It's hard to imagine a more high-profile debut. Hotelier André Balazs,

himself something of a radical, brought ROY on board to help with a hotel project that would definitely see the light of day. Even though it's a budget hotel, QT became the talk of Manhattan and made the precious *Condé Nast Traveller* 'Hot List' before it was even fully open.

Having opened the Mercer in New York and revitalised the Raleigh in South Beach, Miami, André Balazs now rivals Ian Schrager in his ability to create well-designed and much-talked-about hotels that provide a haven for celebs and trendsetters. He has moved into the middle market with his Standard chain, and further towards cheap-chic with QT, which he has jokingly referred to as 'sub-Standard'. It's not. Converted from an office block just off Times Square, it's a no-frills hotel with small rooms (ranging from 17 to 25 square metres), but it's brimming with youthful media and fashion cognoscenti who are looking for style on a low budget. Part of the lure is the combination of location and price (doubles start at just $125, with 25 per cent discount for under-25s), but its quirkiness will mean that it should become loved, and not just useful. As the name implies, it's knowingly but humorously cool. As well as telling the world it's a 'cutie', it draws its name from *On the QT* (i.e. 'on the quiet'), the witty, salacious gossip magazine from the 1950s and 1960s that gloried in headlines such as 'The plot to make lesbianism smart' and 'Did the Reds flip Frances Farmer?' For the uninitiated, a collage of its sensational stories forms part of the hotel décor.

The design may not compare with the startling innovation of ROY's unrealised hotels, but it still has a few appealing little shockers up its sleeve. A small swimming pool sits in the middle of the lobby. Along one side, the wall includes the glazed bottle display of the lobby bar that is situated in an adjoining room, so swimmers can look beyond the edge of the water and see straight into the bar, while drinkers can get glimpses of the water-show. For those who would rather have a closer inspection of the pool antics, one side of the pool also has a terrace of seats. A nightly DJ adds to the full-on, see-and-be-seen atmosphere, and the pool has

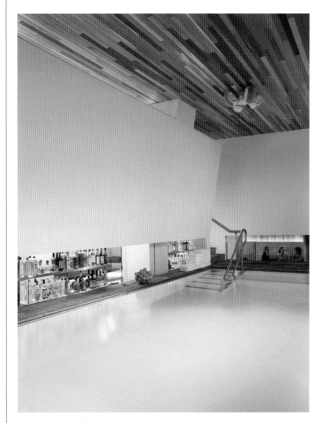

Above and opposite: **Hotel QT, New York**. The cedar-clad lobby features a small pool and views into the adjoining bar. QT may be a budget hotel, but it's flowing with NY-style confidence

Hotel name	QT
Address	125 West 45th Street, New York, NY 10036, USA
Telephone	+1 212 354 2323
Website	www.hotelqt.com
Design style	Budget hotel mixes New York confidence with Scandinavian style
No. of rooms	140 rooms
Bars and restaurants	Lobby bar
Spa facilities	Lobby pool; gym with steam room and sauna
Clientele	Young, hip bunk-bed lovers

underwater speakers. Throughout the hotel, the colours are light and the design seems to be Scandinavian-influenced: bleached woods, stone, white linen and pinks help to evoke a natural, airy atmosphere in the restricted spaces. The lobby is clad with light cedar, and the bar has cork stools along with pink banquettes covered with mohair and leather.

Upstairs, another element that has got NY scenesters chattering is the bunks and platform beds. One of the family rooms has a small bed suspended by poles above a queen-size bed. Others have four bunk beds, providing a retro trip for friends who grew up with too many siblings in small houses. Details such as white Egyptian-cotton bed linen, unusual lights, flat-screen televisions, high-speed internet access points and mini-refrigerators help ensure that QT doesn't feel like a hostel. In order to maximise space, all the furniture except for a small table and chair is built-in, with the bed plinth providing storage space and extending to form flat bedside surfaces.

There have been shortcuts, of course, such as a check-in kiosk instead of a reception and no room service. The mini-fridge is empty – if guests want to extend the party after the pool area's gone quiet, they have to purchase their tipple of choice from the kiosk. Still, it's a small price to pay.

Above: **Hotel QT, New York.** Light colours and incorporated furniture are used to make the most of the small rooms

Above: Hotel QT, New York. The bar, also clad with cedar wood, has high-backed banquettes and an open, communal feel that has proved a hit with New Yorkers

Left: Hotel QT, New York. One of the hotel's talking points has been the family rooms, featuring single beds suspended over doubles, while there are also bunk-bed options

Below: Hotel QT, New York. Low cost, high style. André Balazs and Lindy Roy's attention to detail should ensure that QT proves to be more than a passing fad

convert

Progress is littered with casualties, but hotel culture always seems to be able to embrace it positively. The bright jewel of change leads to the discarding of the old and this can have a terrible effect on the physical environment – technological advances, changes in manufacturing techniques and alterations in lifestyle can rip the heart out of a city. The power of banking now lies in the ether, rather than the grand, high-ceilinged buildings of yesterday; small shops close in the face of competition from hypermarkets and the internet; technology reduces the number of staff and can leave large, inner-city office buildings redundant. The Second World War may have left gap-toothed streets, but the recent speed of change has brought its own casualties, leaving buildings to rot where they stand. The disused buildings in more historical cities may be disintegrating, but they are often protected from demolition or significant alteration which could improve the chances of re-use. At the same time, tourism is undimmed and it seems integral to modern aspirations. It rides on the back of lifestyle changes and technological advances, but is yet to become significantly 'virtual'. The rise in travel has led to a demand for new hotels, but the space of major, popular cities is so compressed that there is little possibility for new buildings (when the 460-room City Inn Westminster opened in 2003, it was the largest new hotel built in London for 30 years). Fortunately, hotel culture has shown an incredible flexibility for adapting and re-using grand and interesting buildings, bringing them back to life with a purpose that meets the new age.

Architects and designers, not usually known as a happy bunch, seem to glory in the restrictions and restraints of conversion. Many of the best-designed hotels of recent years are converted from factories, offices and

convert

warehouses that have been left behind by time. The fashion designer Christian Lacroix has turned the oldest bakery in Paris into the city's newest hip hotel, the Petit Moulin. He was inspired by scraps of old wallpaper, the original staircase and the warren of small rooms which is the antithesis of modern spatial requirements, and the result is surely finer than something that he would have created from a blank sheet or screen. Elsewhere, Marcel Wanders has designed the highly unusual Lute Suites from the impractically small workers' cottages attached to a disused gunpowder factory. Banks, warehouses and courthouses have also been used to give varying degrees of historical texture, wit and irony to environments that still respond to the modern concept of the hotel. In Buenos Aires, Alan Faena and Philippe Starck have gone one step further, allowing a building from the past to become a positive symbol of the city's future.

Some of the projects included in other chapters of this book are also conversions, particularly in the Retreat & Refresh chapter, which focuses on the re-use of English country houses but also includes the integration of an old convent facade, along with the adaptation of the headquarters of a fabric company and the house of a Bhutanese nobleman.

There are many other genres of building that I have not included here which are being used to fuel the growth of the tourism industry. Primarily these have already existed as a type of accommodation, which often makes their conversion less architecturally interesting, but nonetheless points to a shift in the social and cultural fabric of society. An entire book could be dedicated to the hotel conversion of monasteries, seminaries, churches and convents. Ironically, while a genre of hotel culture is exploding on the back of a contemporary desire for spirituality, meditation and holistic wellbeing, hotels are taking over the now redundant facilities of organised religion. This is symptomatic of a popular desire both to revel in the intensified pleasures of modern life and to wish to withdraw from its intensified pressure and superficial commercialism. It's a very modern paradox, but, as ever, the hotel industry reacts pragmatically, using and reusing materials and structures, and redefining services and environments, to meet a shift in culture. This ability to understand, or pre-empt, a change in social fabric and the consequent structural connotations has been combined with the aesthetically orientated vision of designers to ratchet up the significance of hotel style.

Left: **Lute Suites, Ouderkerk**. Suite 5's bubble bathtub, beside a tiled photographic image, provides views of the former gunpowder factory

Hôtel du Petit Moulin

Christian Lacroix

Location: **Paris**
Completion date: **2005**

As hotel design has become so central to our understanding and appreciation of style, it's no surprise that the leaders of world fashion have increasingly become involved in hotel interiors. Antonio Miró, John Rocha and now Christian Lacroix have all undertaken hotel projects in recent years. It *is* quite surprising that so many of them are actually good at hotel design, that a fresh approach to couture really can extend to the creation of a whole environment. It may be a relatively small leap from designing print patterns to choosing wallpaper, but hotel design is a specialism beleaguered by restraints: style, functionalism and structure have to be married in an endless list of often mundane considerations from mixer taps to the use of frosted glass or the height of a bar counter. Part of the trick of hotel

design is sustaining an intangible psychological benefit: the guests must feel secure within a luxurious refuge from the city or from their normal lives. Chinks in the design or a functional failure soon vaporise the magic.

Christian Lacroix has been a significant name in world fashion for 20 years and has extended his success into perfumery, jewellery and theatre costume design. He has drawn on his knowledge of the latter for this step into hotel interiors, saying that the design lies 'between fashion and theatre'. The Hôtel du Petit Moulin is a joyous, satisfying, multi-layered Parisian refuge that he has orchestrated despite the added handicap of working on a building that is registered as an historic monument. To create the hotel, architects Cabinet Vincent Bastie conjoined two old buildings, one of which housed the oldest bakery in Paris, supposedly frequented by Victor Hugo. The bakery was built in the 17th century but it is the boulangerie shopfront and sign, dating from 1900, that have preserved status. The traditional gold lettering and etched windows make an alluring disguise for the hotel, helping to declare from the outset that Lacroix's interior will be highly distinctive. Behind the facade, the whole building has been renovated, but the history of the site and the atmosphere of old Paris have not been stripped away. Lacroix, who lives nearby, was captivated by the building's past, its 17th-century staircase and unusual perspectives, and chose to use its warren of hallways and rooms to evoke different aspects of the enduringly cool Marais district.

The extravagance of Lacroix's couture has transferred to the 17 individually designed en-suite rooms – perhaps this is one hotel that can be genuinely called 'boutique'. The furniture is a blend of antique and contemporary classics, often juxtaposed with prints and fabrics. A red Arne Jacobsen 'Swan' chair is framed by wallpaper depicting traditional scenes of life on the waterways; a plain green leather headboard rests against huge, colourful sketches of dress designs. The effect is

Above: Hôtel du Petit Moulin, Paris. Each of the 17 en-suite rooms is individually designed. For this bedroom, Christian Lacroix draws directly from his work as a fashion designer

Opposite: Hôtel du Petit Moulin, Paris. The hotel has been created from two buildings, including a 17th-century bakery. The listed shopfront, dating from 1900, now reveals the hotel's reception

Hotel name	Hôtel du Petit Moulin
Address	29–31 rue du Poitou, 75003 Paris, France
Telephone	+33 (0)1 42 74 10 10
Website	www.paris-hotel-petitmoulin.com
Design style	An exuberant trip through the chambers of a fashion designer's mind
No. of rooms	17 rooms
Bars and restaurants	Private bar for guests
Spa facilities	None
Clientele	Art-lovers drawn to the Marais' museums and galleries

that of a doll's house brimming with a jumble of all the ideas, textures and styles that have emboldened a long, varied career in fashion. It seems as if the designer's sketchpad has been randomly riffled through and pasted on the walls, and the resulting unique and varied papers and frescoes set the tone for each room. Influences range from full-on kitsch (a heart-shaped Venetian mirror is surrounded by blood-red tiles in one of the bathrooms) to masculine Zen minimalism and Pop Art. Flooring varies from shag carpets and polka-dot stairwells to Provençal tiles, with fabrics including Jouy linens, Scandinavian textiles, leather, velvet and taffeta.

Consequently, the design will have to put up with the 'eclectic' label, but it is spurred on by a desire to mirror the diversity of the Marais rather than by an ill-conceived wish to mix-and-match. The result is humorous and inviting. This may be one man's idiosyncratic creation, but at all times the design seems to be undertaken as an intimate discourse with the guest and their own memories and associations.

Modern-day luxuries and expectations are catered for with each room having good lighting, a well-equipped bathroom, air conditioning, flat-screen television, wireless internet access, minibar and personal safe.

Opposite: **Hôtel du Petit Moulin, Paris.** A heart-shaped Venetian mirror adds a touch of camp sumptuousness to this blood-red tiled bathroom

Above and below: **Hôtel du Petit Moulin, Paris.** The individual atmosphere of each room is drawn from the unusual wall panels and wallpapers

Opposite: **Hôtel du Petit Moulin, Paris.** Colours
and textures are constantly juxtaposed: a black-
lacquered door leads from a red-and-gold striped
room to a green stairwell featuring a polka-dot carpet

Above: **Hôtel du Petit Moulin, Paris.** The seating
in the hotel's private bar includes classic 1960s
designs such as Pierre Paulin's 'Little Tulip' chairs

Lute Suites

Marcel Wanders

Location: **Ouderkerk**
Completion date: **2005**

All too often, analogies are made between architecture and music, but despite the name Lute Suites has little to do with Bach, and everything to do with the vision of the bold and original designer Marcel Wanders and the restaurateur Peter Lute. However, it's fair – if a little trite – to say that their creation is a series of variations. Peter and Marieke Lute opened a contemporary, French-influenced restaurant in Ouderkerk, just south of Amsterdam, in 2002, but their ambitions soon stretched to augmenting it with a new hotel concept. In fact, Peter Lute does not call it a hotel at all. It is seven individual, luxury suites in a series of workers' cottages overlooking the Amstel river. The conventional hotel concept will become even more fragmented into disparate units with the addition of a further three suites dotted around Amsterdam; the intention is for Lute Suites to become a city-wide project that is not tied to a specific location.

Marcel Wanders emerged out of the heralded Droog group to reach international status with unconventional, often witty designs for Moooi, Kartell, Flos, Cappellini and Bisazza. He recently designed the lobby, bar and restaurant for Hotel on Rivington, one of the very few genuinely interesting new hotels to open in the United States in the last few years. The Wanders/Lute partnership began when the designer came to eat in the restaurant, which had been converted from a large building that was part of an 18th-century gunpowder factory. The nearby workers' cottagers, dating from 1740, proved an irresistible lure for their mutual taste for innovation. All the suites are double, with their own entrance, and the cottages' narrow, perpendicular shape and gable was used to present separate living rooms, bathrooms and bedrooms. If there is a linking theme to each uniquely designed suite, it is found in the natural motifs and mosaics, some of which are drawn from Wanders and Bisazza's aptly named 'One morning they woke up …' range: Suite 1 has a Bisazza snowflake wall, the bathroom wall of Suite 6 has a black-and-white nature pattern, and the inlaid metal floor of Suite 5's living room features large, patterned hexagons. Antiques and chandeliers are merged with contemporary furnishings, painted or inlaid floors, Corian baths and glass partitions.

In Suite 7, the entrance hallway has a metal inlaid floor, leading to a spiral staircase. To the right, a smoked-glass wall reveals a bathroom blending modern Boffi fittings, an antique washstand and mirror, and a red-and-white tiled shower. To the left, amorphous forms emerge from the white wall of the living room, where golden chandeliers, encased in tubes, hang above a colourful, pod-like, mosaic side table. Up the spiral staircase, the bedroom's gable wall is covered with soft, studded upholstery, while the lampshades are supported by Wanders-designed 'one-minute sculptures' in the form of beaten, gold-coloured animals. A couple of the suites, such as number 3, are smaller, covering only 40 square

Left: Lute Suites, Ouderkerk. Each of the seven suites is in an individual house, converted from 18th-century cottages. In Suite 2, unusual furniture, such as Marcel Wanders' colourful Bisazza mosaic side table and an integrated desk/chair, stands on lime-green floorboards

Opposite: Lute Suites, Ouderkerk. A bell-shaped gable stands above the entrance passageway of the former gunpowder factory

Hotel name	Lute Suites
Address	Amsteldijk Zuid 54–58, 1184 VD Ouderkerk a/d Amstel, The Netherlands
Telephone	+31 (0)20 47 22 462
Website	www.lutesuites.com
Design style	18th-century gabled cottages housing Wander's mosaic and metal vision
No. of rooms	7 suites
Bars and restaurants	Lute Restaurant
Spa facilities	None
Clientele	Design-crazy tourists and imaginative business people

metres rather than the usual 70, but compensations include a gold ceiling and baroque wallpaper.

Breakfast can be brought to the door, but room service doesn't really exist as the emphasis of Lute Suites is upon individual environments rather than hotel services. Guests can cook in their own small kitchenette, or choose to eat in the restaurant, one of the two boardrooms, or in local cafés. The boardrooms are ideal for meetings: it is envisaged that the suites will be rented by businesspeople as well as tourists, and Wanders wanted to make sure they had stylish facilities rather than having negotiations while perching on the edge of boutique-hotel beds.

The three additional Lute ventures will have very promising locations for tourists, variously situated close to Dam Square and the Royal Palace; near the Van Gogh Museum; and on canal houseboats. In the meantime, Lute Suites, set in the flatlands of Noord-Holland, has to lure guests to Ouderkerk with the promise of excellent design and good food. Luckily, the suites are situated next to a Vitra outlet, helping make Ouderkerk an unlikely destination for design aficionados. For those who tire of looking at the Ron Arad, Jasper Morrison and Philippe Starck furniture designs and the vast skies, Peter's father runs a 1920s canal boat up the Amstel to Amsterdam.

Above: **Lute Suites, Ouderkerk.** The top of the cottage gable has been converted into a loft for Suite 5's 'sleeping nook' bedroom

Right: **Lute Suites, Ouderkerk.** The inlaid metal floor and Marcel Wanders-designed wallpaper both incorporate a hexagonal motif in the living room of Suite 5

Above: **Lute Suites, Ouderkerk.** The metal inlaid flooring of Suite 7's hallway leads to the spiral staircase, with the glass wall of the bathroom on the right

Right: **Lute Suites, Ouderkerk.** Golden chandeliers hang between the rafters in Suite 7. The floral mosaic table provides the other colouring

Right: **Lute Suites, Ouderkerk.** The gable wall of Suite 7's bedroom is padded, acting as a headboard. There are golden lamp bases in the shape of animals on either side of the bed

Above: Lute Suites, Ouderkerk. Suite 3 is one of the smaller spaces. The bathroom facilities are incorporated into the bedroom

Opposite: Lute Suites, Ouderkerk. One of the two boardrooms, featuring Wanders' 'VIP' chairs. They incorporate wireless internet access, DVD players and LCD screens

Far left and left: Lute Suites, Ouderkerk. Drawings for individual suites. Even though they at first seem very conceptual, the finished designs are remarkably similar

Faena Hotel + Universe

Philippe Starck

Location: **Buenos Aires**
Completion date: **2004**

Argentina has taken something of a beating over the last few years, with 2001–3's hyper-inflation undermining both the welfare and the natural confidence of the people. At least it didn't reach the scale of the 5,000 per cent price index rise that occurred in a single year in the 1980s. Such instability, though, hardly provided the right environment for hotel investment, and the country remained largely uninvolved in the luxury, designer hotel renaissance that has swept across so much of the world. Finally, fashion designer and entrepreneur Alan Faena stuck his head above the parapet and decided that not only should Buenos Aires have a contemporary hotel created by the world's most famous hotel designer, but that the hotel should offer a new level of hospitality experience. It would also provide Philippe Starck with a chance to show the world that there was life after Ian Schrager, his erstwhile hotel partner.

The name of the hotel is bold. The 'Universe' refers to all the additional services and amenities linked to the hotel, including a swimming pool and bar, 80 private apartments, El Cabaret theatre space, El Living music room, library and bar, the Laboratory of Experimental Artists, restaurants and a hammam, spa and gym. Faena calls it 'a cultural centre that has a hotel in it', and wishes it to provide part of the social texture of Argentina. Therefore, it is fitting that the complex is housed in a former grain warehouse, dating from 1902 and known as El Porteño, which is the name used to describe people from Buenos Aires. The stern brick edifice gives little suggestion of Starck's interior, which combines rococo and contemporary styles but is infused with a dark passion which is typically Argentinian and very removed from Starck's usual use of light-coloured backdrops. Rich, dark woods, deep reds and gold create an opulent scenario. The entrance is monumental: the 80-metre-long aisle, known as La Catedral, soars upwards with the exposed brickwork swathed with shimmering gold curtains. A red carpet and elongated benches extenuate the length. El Mercado restaurant and El Living are also full of deep reds and browns, and the local culture shows its influence through the presence of antlers and cowhide rugs. Starck's use of unusual objects and furniture seems more at ease within this dark setting than in some of his other interiors, where the items can seem so starkly isolated that it requires nerve to sit on them in any comfort.

Other parts of the complex are lighter. El Bistro restaurant is almost entirely white, with delicate red and gold touches. Unicorn heads emerge from between the

Above: Faena Hotel + Universe, Buenos Aires. La Catedral is a monumental entranceway, with the exposed brickwork dressed with long, golden drapes

Opposite: Faena Hotel + Universe, Buenos Aires. The converted grain silo, dating from 1902, is situated in the redeveloped Puerto Madero Este docklands. The complex houses the hotel, private apartments, restaurants, a gallery and shops

Hotel name	Faena Hotel + Universe
Address	Martha Salotti 445, Buenos Aires C1107CMB, Argentina
Telephone	+54 (0)11 4010 9000 or design hotels™ 00800 37 46 83 57
Website	www.faenahotelanduniverse.com
Design style	Imperial Starck infused with Argentinian passion
No. of rooms	85 rooms and suites, including 2 presidential suites
Bars and restaurants	El Living lounge bar; Pool Bar; El Mercado restaurant; El Bistro restaurant
Spa facilities	Gym-Spa-Hammam offering massages, beauty treatments, Turkish bath
Clientele	Sophisticated travellers and high-class local revellers

white curtains, adding a touch of eccentricity. The guestrooms are a relatively classic depiction of the Empire style mixed with Starck's signature items such as glass bathrooms and gilt, swan-armed chairs. The white walls and furniture add a serene quality amongst the red velvet curtains and red-and-gold rugs. Materials are luxurious, including marble, crystal, etched glass, and lapacho-wood floorboards, while each room also has the full range of modern indulgences.

The real departure for Faena Hotel + Universe is provided by its 'experiences', which offer the chance to become embroiled in Argentinian culture. The guests do not check in at reception – they are met by their own personal 'Experience Manager' who provides the services of butler, concierge and personal assistant. The manager can organise a wide range of experiences, including trips to famous tango *milongas*, an art and antiques tour, wine tasting, polo matches, or a photography excursion. At each experience, you are placed in the hands of a local expert. The combination of high design and individual attention means that the Faena Hotel strikes a very contemporary balance as it attempts to re-evoke the past glories of Argentinian culture. International jet-setters are already arriving to 'pampa' themselves and the hotel has won Best New Hotel at the *Wallpaper** Design Awards for 2004.

Right: Faena Hotel + Universe, Buenos Aires. While many of the interiors feature dark reds, browns and exposed brickwork, El Bistro restaurant is almost entirely white. Wall-mounted unicorn heads add a curious mythological touch

Opposite: Faena Hotel + Universe, Buenos Aires.. El Living is a lounge, library and bar with traditional leather furniture and wooden flooring

Below: Faena Hotel + Universe, Buenos Aires. Traditional European markets and cantinas inspire El Mercado restaurant

Right: **Faena Hotel + Universe, Buenos Aires.**
The pool, with its own bar pavilion, is proving to be
a favourite place amongst the guests

Opposite and right: **Faena Hotel + Universe,
Buenos Aires.** The Empire-style guestrooms have
white upholstered beds with gold feet, large, glass
bathrooms and red velvet curtains

The Zetter Restaurant & Rooms

Precious McBane/ Chetwood Associates

Location: **London**
Completion date: **2004**

In recent years, more hotels have woken up to the benefits of having a stand-alone, high-quality restaurant which succeeds far beyond the provision of fodder for unadventurous guests. Good-quality restaurants and bars add kudos to a hotel, as well as providing a regular, locally generated income during low season. The entwining of accommodation and catering has been such that the restaurant now forms a large part of the critical expectations of a high-concept hotel design. The ever-burgeoning lifestyle cognoscenti arrive almost before any guests, trying out the cocktails and menu rather than the beds. More than ever, radical hoteliers are encroaching on the market of restaurateurs, but a fight back has begun. Successful restaurateurs are entering the hotel market, allying their experience of creating unique entertainment spaces with the broader concept of the design hotel. In Barcelona, Grupo Tragaluz has built Omm upon its reputation for stylish restaurants. In London, Michael Benyan and Mark Sainsbury, who between them have been involved in the success of Moro, The Quality Chop House, the Union Café and Kensington Place, have created The Zetter Restaurant & Rooms.

The Zetter looks both forward and back in creating an establishment which ably meets current passions. The owners call The Zetter an 'urban inn', highlighting the ancient wayfarer's need for both refreshment and hotel facilities. The location and building were key. Clerkenwell is a fascinating district with a history dating back to the 12th century. Despite its proximity to the very heart of London, it had become a largely neglected area until it was 'rediscovered' by young, artistic urbanites in the 1990s. Empty, derelict or uninspiring premises were overhauled as the district quickly became awash with cool bars, restaurants and clubs. Interestingly, though, there are hardly any hotels catering for outside visitors to this new media-Mecca. Benyan and Sainsbury have worked a new niche with their conversion of a 19th-century warehouse, the former home to the family-run betting company Zetter's Pools.

The building is as graceful a Victorian warehouse as you are likely to find, with golden brickwork and, all-importantly, a great many large windows. The work of Chetwood Associates has been very sympathetic to the original exterior, restoring its giant sash windows and ensuring that it blends in with the local architecture. Even the hotel signage is restrained (a small red 'Z' stands at the top of the building), but pink neon strips shining from the top of the window casements indicate that the warehouse has a new, funkier purpose. The *tour de force*

Above: The Zetter, London. The hotel has been sensitively converted from a 19th-century warehouse which curves onto St John's Square in Clerkenwell

Opposite: The Zetter, London. The bar sits at the base of a new, five-storey atrium, around which are the walkways to the bedrooms. The wood-panelled room houses red tables and 'Little Tulip' chairs covered in a surprising floral pattern

Hotel name	The Zetter Restaurant & Rooms
Address	86–88 Clerkenwell Road, London EC1M 5RJ, UK
Telephone	+44 (0)20 7324 4444
Website	www.thezetter.com
Design style	Contemporary and heritage mix in a Victorian warehouse
No. of rooms	59 rooms, including 7 rooftop studios
Bars and restaurants	The Zetter bar and modern Italian restaurant, open from breakfast to dinner
Spa facilities	None
Clientele	Youthful style-cognoscenti drawn to Clerkenwell's nightlife

of the conversion is inside, where a new atrium runs up through the centre of the building's five floors, creating a semicircular lightwell which is punctuated by the circular walkways that lead to the 59 rooms. The alienation caused by straight, neon-lit hotel corridors has been done away with. Chetwood Associates has also managed to integrate a new top floor, allowing for seven rooftop suites, without raising the overall height of the building.

The atrium brings natural light into the bar, a curving, wood-panelled room that sits at its base. This features a woven, floral Axminster carpet whose muted colours complement the covers on Pierre Paulin's classic 'Little Tulip' chairs. There is a hatch in the panelling so drinkers need not go around to the restaurant's bar counter for service. The restaurant itself, serving modern Italian food, is both relaxed and hugely successful. As intended, it feels like the buzzing core of the hotel. It has a black marble bar, oversized black lampshades and black dining chairs, but it is otherwise designed to be simple, bright and airy.

In the rest of the hotel, interior designers Precious McBane have made a grander design statement. Even

the stairs and lift have a high impact through the use of red patterns. The rooms have a variety of layouts and colour schemes but all feature a mix of contemporary and classic furniture, including Walter Knoll 'Flow' armchairs in a vibrant pink floral pattern, colourful bespoke blankets featuring the 'Z' monogram and very effective mood-lighting. The rooftop studios have private terraces with great views of London, and follow the curve of the building's facade, giving each a distinctive shape. Second-hand Penguin paperbacks offer classic entertainment but all the rooms are fitted with the latest technology, with flat-screen, interactive televisions offering movies-on-demand and a library of 4,000 music tracks. With weekend room rates at only just over £100, The Zetter is keen to offer a combination of services, design and price that appeals to the young style-lovers who flood into Clerkenwell's bars and clubs.

The Zetter also has eco-credentials, with a high use of sustainable materials. Re-evoking Clerkenwell's past fame as a spa area, the hotel bottles its own water from a 450-metre borehole which is also used to feed the air-cooling system.

Opposite: **The Zetter, London.** The black-and-white-themed restaurant is the heart of the enterprise, as implied by its full name, The Zetter Restaurant & Rooms

Right and below: **The Zetter, London.** Traditional furniture is invigorated with unusual materials throughout the rooms and studios

Left and above: **The Zetter, London.** Both the lift and the staircase up to the rooms have bold red and silver designs

Opposite: **The Zetter, London.** The rooms have different colour schemes, supported by the wash of mood-lighting. The 'Flow' chairs in this pink rooftop studio are given a makeover that reflects the design's constant blend of heritage and modernity

Above: **The Zetter, London.** An extra floor for seven rooftop studios was incorporated into the conversion. The floor-to-ceiling glazing and private terraces emphasise the views

Aleph
Adam D Tihany

Location: **Rome**
Completion date: **2003**

If the love of money is the root of all evil, then it is fitting that Adam D Tihany's conversion of the headquarters of the Italian bank Istituto Credito Casse di Risparmio Italiane is partially inspired by Dante's *Inferno*. The new Aleph hotel's lobby and reception, which highlight the bank's marble staircase and wooden panels, blaze with crimson. However, this is a very sultry idea of hell and elsewhere in the hotel the more heavenly aspects of *The Divine Comedy* take over.

The former bank is situated just by central Rome's Via Veneto in a five-storey building finished in 1931. The location and some of the remaining decorative features made it perfect for a £15 million conversion into a high-class hotel for the Boscolo brothers. With other ventures including the Exedra, converted from a papal granary in Rome, and the Dei Dogi, a former embassy in Venice, they have become expert in turning historically interesting buildings into hotels. Tihany is one of the world's foremost restaurant designers, responsible for New York's Le Cirque, but while he has created many top-hotel dining rooms and bars, he undertakes whole hotel commissions quite rarely. According to him, 'the Aleph is not a place to stay – it's a state of mind'. That state is heaven and hell, and the paradoxical merging of the two which Tihany calls the essence of Rome. The areas may be called 'Sin' or 'Paradise', but it's up to the guest to find paradise in hell or the devil in heaven. Such an idea could easily tire or falter, but the designer has a mastery of details which gives a depth to the broad sway of the concept.

The limestone facade of the bank remains largely unadulterated but the red rectangle in the centre of the entranceway's glass doors introduces the devilish theme of the interior transformation. Inside, two large samurai statues and a polished black granite floor, broken up with red mosaic rectangles, lead the way to the reception desk as if marking the route to the gates of hell. The desk itself is authoritative, with a white Corian desk and overhang, but not threatening. It is almost the sole suggestion of purity on a ground floor of amenities dedicated to decadence and collectively known as 'Sin'.

Another temple of goodness is the Angelo bar, which also has a white Corian counter, but this is surrounded by the lounge's dark maze of black-and-red furnishings, including red-leather bar stools, stained mahogany panels, and crimson upholstery. The mirrored, cubic tables are decorated as dice: Tihany is daring the guests to gamble with their souls. He has even turned the floor of the black-and-red interior courtyard into a huge backgammon board, above which are two dice, suspended in mid-throw. At the rear of the ground floor

Above: **Aleph, Rome.** The designer has delighted in creating a luxurious, pleasurable version of hell. The lounge is panelled with red-stained mahogany and the furniture is a mix of red and black textures and materials

Opposite: **Aleph, Rome.** The entranceway to Adam D Tihany's design, inspired by Dante's *The Divine Comedy*. Some features of the former bank headquarters, such as the marble staircase, remain

Hotel name	Aleph
Address	Via di San Basilio 15, 00187 Rome, Italy
Telephone	+39 06 422 901
Website	www.boscolohotels.com
Design style	Dante's *The Divine Comedy* brought to tempting life
No. of rooms	96 rooms, including 32 deluxe rooms, 4 junior suites, 2 suites
Bars and restaurants	Maremoto restaurant; Dioniso Wine Bar, Angelo Bar; 7 Heaven terrace bar & restaurant
Spa facilities	Paradise Spa with sauna; Turkish bath, thermal pool; gym; and treatments including melted chocolate massage, honey body scrub with maize flour, and Chinese reflexology
Clientele	Lovers of decadence who want to dice with the devil

the Maremoto restaurant has red-backed glass tables and red-leather banquettes – even the goblet glasses and crockery carry the blood-red theme. As the name suggests, the panelled Red Library is another homage to monochrome, but, surprisingly, not to books: the shelves of titles are just illuminated virtual images.

In a reversal of normal structures, Paradise, as the spa is named, is found below hell. Situated in the basement, through the original bank-vault door, the luscious red motif is given over to spa-friendly blue, silver and white hues and clean materials. Upstairs, the 96 bedrooms are light, with a tranquil blue and ivory scheme: in Tihany's design, blood and passion seem exclusively to reside in the public arena. Venetian-glass sconces, white furniture and pale woods offer a rather ordered, serene luxury. However, the fabric of the Eternal City and the history of the building are not forgotten. The furniture is 1930s Italian, while Brian Tihany, the designer's son, has created a range of huge photographic murals of Roman streets, alleys and piazzas. These are very striking, especially when set into the corner of a room to create a trompe l'oeil. The hotel offers other views of Rome – real this time – from the 7 Heaven restaurant and bar on an open terrace. The heavenly theme rules here, with globe lights and soft, deep, white chairs.

Above: Aleph, Rome. Angelic white makes a rare appearance on the ground floor, with the Angelo Bar's white Corian counter battling against the crimson flow

Below: Aleph, Rome. The 'Sin' area's restaurant continues the devilish red-and-black theme, right through to the crockery and glassware

Right: Aleph, Rome. Giant dice are suspended mid-throw above a huge backgammon board in the hotel's interior courtyard. Guests are lured into throwing caution to the wind in Tihany's decadent design

Below: Aleph, Rome. The Red Library's books are illuminated virtual images

Left: **Aleph, Rome.** The terrace provides heavenly views of the Eternal City

Below: **Aleph, Rome.** A third of the 96 guest rooms are deluxe. Ivory and blue themes create a serene atmosphere in deliberate contrast to the vibrant red heart of the hotel. Brian Tihany's photographic murals of Rome create interesting trompe l'oeils

Left: Aleph, Rome. The suite bathrooms are strictly modern, with clear Perspex basins, steel fittings and light wood

Left: Aleph, Rome. Italian craftsmanship is celebrated in the use of glass, mirrors and 1930s furniture

Courthouse Hotel Kempinski

Sunita Sanger and Ward Design Services

Location: **London**
Completion date: **2005**

The Courthouse on central London's Great Marlborough Street has great historical significance, especially for voyeurs of celebrity crime. As a magistrates' court, the building has provided the setting for notorious proceedings involving Oscar Wilde, John Profumo and the Rolling Stones' Mick Jagger and Keith Richards. When the Sanger family's Surejogi Hotels chose to turn the building into a hotel, they decided to allow it to revel in its history. Sunita Sanger herself has overseen the conversion of the interior, and has glorified many of the original features, but their new context has added a sense of fun and humour rather than staid reverence.

The Grade II-listed, sandstone exterior looks much as it did when the court closed in 2000, except that it is now very clean and well lit, but it hides a £20 million conversion which tripled the building's size. The social spaces, located within the original building, provide the showpieces. The bar is simply called The Bar, reflecting the previous use of the space rather than a lack of imagination, and includes three original prison cells that are now private booths. The entrance to the bar, at the end of a long lounge, is through iron gates, while iron bars also grace the internal windows. The main space is coyly austere, with black-and-white leather seating, Fernhill stone-clad walls and slate flooring. The three cell-booths have cast-iron prison doors and foreboding, institutional whitewash covering the brickwork. However, former internees who liked the finer things in life will be pleased to note that the hard benches are now covered in comfortable cushions, and the toilet bowl (still standing in the corner but presumably now safely sanitised) holds an ice bucket.

The Number One Court, also on the ground floor, is the Silk restaurant. Beneath a vaulted glass ceiling, the original oak panelling, benches, witness stand and dock all remain – if the space weren't dotted with white chairs and tables, it would look much as it must have done during those celebrity trials. Single diners can choose to overlook the room from the witness stand and imagine Oscar Wilde's ill-advised attempt to sue the Marquess of Queensberry for libel, which resulted in his own trial for gross indecency. The trial over the exhibition of John Lennon's seemingly 'obscene' drawings also took place here.

The social spaces share a combination of restraint and touches of exuberance. The yellow-painted Carnaby restaurant, which has its own street-level entrance, features a bent-propeller ceiling light while the formal reception has

Above: Courthouse Hotel Kempinski, London.
The brasserie-style Carnaby restaurant offers
Continental-style fare in crisp surroundings

Opposite: Courthouse Hotel Kempinski, London.
The sandstone facade of Great Marlborough Street
Magistrates' Court is largely unaltered but now hides
the five above-ground storeys of the new hotel

Hotel name	Courthouse Hotel Kempinski
Address	19–21 Great Marlborough Street, London W1F 7HL, UK
Telephone	+44 (0)20 7297 5555
Website	www.courthouse-hotel.com
Design style	Home-from-home for legal eagles (and prisoners)
No. of rooms	103 rooms, 13 suites including 1 penthouse
Bars and restaurants	Silk (with cuisine inspired by the Silk Route), Carnaby (international cuisine) and The Waiting Room (breakfast/snacks) restaurants; The Bar
Spa facilities	Sanook spa: treatment rooms, sonarium, steam showers, indoor swimming pool and gym
Clientele	European business people and wealthy tourists. The weekday bar and restaurant clientele is made up of local media-workers

shell-shaped chairs beneath a Murano chandelier. Beyond the reception, the adaptable lounge area is quite subdued but has illuminated, glass-encased water features reaching upwards from heavy, marble-cast pots.

The standard rooms are situated in the new wing, built on the site of a police station and shooting range, and have either dark or light colour schemes. They are decorated in a smart, restrained style that is typical of the expanding Kempinski chain, which manages both the Courthouse and Bentley hotels for the Sanger family. The suites, though, are in the judges' robing rooms on the original building's first floor. As well as four-poster beds, some of the suites have Robert Adam fireplaces. The penthouse Lalique Suite (available for £2,500 per night) was the former residence of the Metropolitan Police Commissioner, and, as the name implies, it is fitted out with Lalique creations from chandeliers and doorknobs to furniture.

The hotel has a spa featuring a square swimming pool, sonarium and hot tub, separated from the gym by a glass wall. One of the two aluminium-walled beauty treatment rooms has a glass floor hanging over the pool. Generally, the hotel is well equipped to meet the demands of the 21st century. Private cinemas are now becoming a regular feature within the 'new' country house hotels and private clubs so beloved of London's medialand. With a location on the shoulder of Soho, the Courthouse is likely to find great use for its own 100-seater auditorium, stylishly fitted out with leather seating, suede walls and an aubergine-coloured carpet. Along with the adaptable lounge and a purpose-designed conference suite, Courthouse Hotel Kempinski is primed for launches and conferences. As far as tourists are concerned, it should also benefit from the Kempinski name, which is very popular amongst German tourists, as well as from its situation opposite Liberty's in the heart of the West End.

Below: **Courthouse Hotel Kempinski, London.** The Number One Court is now the Silk Restaurant. With English oak panelling and the original judges' bench, dock and witness stand, it remains almost exactly as it was when it housed celebrity trials

Right: Courthouse Hotel Kempinski, London.
The cells, with their original cast-iron doors, are now private booths for bar customers. The low partition towards the rear hides the toilet bowl, which can be used to hold an ice bucket. A sign still bears the legend 'Flush WC after use'

Below: Courthouse Hotel Kempinski, London.
Indian mica-slate flooring and Fernhill stone walls lead the way into the main bar space, past three former women's cells on the right

Above: **Courthouse Hotel Kempinski, London.**
Pale-green leather seats and suede walls help make this one of the best private cinema facilities in London

Top: **Courthouse Hotel Kempinski, London.**
The lobby lounge is a large area connecting the reception to the bar. The brown and taupe corduroy sofas and one-piece glass tables can be easily removed to leave a large, adaptable space

Above: **Courthouse Hotel Kempinski, London.**
A 12-arm Murano-glass chandelier hangs over the reception area

Left and below left: **Courthouse Hotel
Kempinski, London.** The room interiors are quite
conservative, but materials do include zebrano-
wood door panels and marble bathrooms. There is
a choice of dark- or light-wood rooms, with both
schemes highlighting the specially designed fabrics

Above: **Courthouse Hotel Kempinski, London.**
The bathroom mirrors are set in the middle of a
frosted picture window, allowing natural light to
come in from the bedroom

eco

Modern-day eco-resorts started to appear back in the 1970s – not long after the first eco-warriors and green parties started to find a political voice – but were very much an unusual, alternative destination. In the last decade or so, with the creation of resorts such as the ground-breaking Kapawi Ecolodge and Reserve in the Amazon rainforest in 1993, they have become much more popular and are now counted as a significant genre in global tourism. There are some ridiculously wild estimates of the current level of ecotourism, but even the more conservative calculations put it at 10 to 15 per cent and growing rapidly. The popularity of the genre is no doubt spurred on by disenchantment with the destructiveness of human 'progress', by unhappiness with the onslaught of materialism and by the dislocation from a genuine relationship with a natural environment. The metropolis is, after all, its own biosphere, its structures a buffer from the chaos of nature. Increasingly, there is a demand for an escape to an unrepressed, less synthetic and purer world, which also mitigates a very personal awakening of the senses.

Despite their gradual increase in popularity, it is fair to say that in design terms, eco-resorts lay in torpor for the first 30 years of their inception. Perhaps the combination of contemporary design and the natural world doesn't suggest itself as a happy marriage. Or perhaps the early ecotourists felt that luxury and ethical worthiness was an uneasy mix. Whatever the combination of reasons, our perception of the eco-resort is usually of the amenity-free hut, where the only luxury is the appeasement of the conscience rather than the pleasures of mind and body. Yet the last few years have seen a revolution in the way we approach ecologically sensitive design. Low-impact tourism no longer means no-impact design. Furthermore, the concept of the eco-resort is finally getting

eco

a foothold in Europe and North America. It is quite shocking that the UK didn't have any ecologically-run hostels until 2005. The UK provides the second highest number of ecotourists worldwide, but has hardly any specific ecologically sound hotel facilities of its own. There has been better progress in Germany where at least the Bleibtreu eco-hotel in Berlin has blended high design and high ethics since 1995. Both the new Vigilius Mountain Resort in the South Tyrol and the Whitepod ski resort in Switzerland point towards a future for European eco-resorts that innovatively combine style and ethics. Hopefully this will mean that European eco-travellers who wish to save the world won't have to burn up the Earth's resources on long-haul flights.

Most of the designs included in this chapter rely on local, natural materials from sustainable sources and are designed to integrate into the natural surroundings. Thatch is used to at least some extent for roofs at both North Island in the Seychelles and Morgan's Rock Hacienda & Ecolodge in Nicaragua, so that at first glance the lodges look like indigenous dwellings. By contrast, Daffonchio & Associates have created a temple of modernism at The Outpost in South Africa, while Matteo Thun's Vigilius Mountain Resort, with its larchwood louvers, looks like nothing seen before. Whitepod, made up of white tent-pods standing on the mountainside, could be mistaken as part of a space exploration programme. Craftily, these designs still manage to be at one with their environments. An ethos of zero or minimal impact is used to enhance the relationship between guest and nature as the boundaries of an abode and its surroundings are cleverly blurred. Exterior walls are often retractable canvas or glazed, while terraces and bathrooms reach out into the natural habitat. All the designs are imbued with a level of detail, and a quality of design and craftsmanship, that appeals to the international, luxury tourist.

So much of modern hotel design is about creating bubbles and microworlds, but in these eco-resorts contemporary designers have managed to explode the dwellings beyond the facades, while at the same time providing textures, comforts and securities that appeal to style gurus and luxury-lovers. They are succeeding in luring mainstream tourists towards ethical solutions in a way that truly indigenous abodes never could.

Below: Morgan's Rock, Playa Ocotal. One of the delights of the bungalows is the swinging daybeds, suspended from the ceiling by ropes and overlooking the forest and bay

Vigilius Mountain Resort

Matteo Thun

Location: **South Tyrol**
Completion date: **2003**

Eco-resorts may have started to spring up in little-populated areas of South America and Africa long ago but, perhaps surprisingly, Europe is now providing the arena for the concentration of new developments. Developers of ski and mountain resorts have finally woken up to the effect that an increase in greenhouse gases is having on their own industry as it ravages natural beauty and curtails the snow season. Typically, now the Europeans are facing up to the situation, the design solutions are proving to be radical.

Vigilius Mountain Resort's eco-credentials begin before arrival. Some ecotourists are galled by the expenditure of aeroplane fuel and the use of 4x4 gas-guzzlers that accompanies their attempts to holiday without damaging nature. It's often more than possible to use up more of the earth's resources on an eco-holiday than by going on a motor vacation or by simply staying in the heart of the city. There are fewer worries at Vigilius, set 1,500 metres up in the Italian Tyrol, as it can be reached only by cable car from Lana, the nearest town. The hotel itself sits amongst the contours of the Vigiljoch in the Dolomites, just over the border from Austria. It inhabits the site of a hotel that was built at the same time as the cable cars were introduced in 1912, but which did not prove to be so enduring.

Vigilius is perhaps the supreme eco-resort, with the beauty of its design matching perfectly its ethical intentions. Consequently, it has already started to win awards ranging from 'ClimateHouse A' ecological categorisation to *Wallpaper**'s Best New Eco Retreat Design Award 2004. Matteo Thun's design lives up to one of his main objectives: that 'the boundaries ... between architecture and nature vanish'. The flat larch-wood structure, which gently curves outwards at one end, is barely visible among the trees. The distinctive horizontal slats that cover the facade prevent the sun from overheating the interior in the summer and give the building a structural frailty that matches the surrounding

tall, thin larch trees. Throughout, there is an emphasis on wood and glass from renewable resources, including the re-use of timber from a 300-year-old barn, while the rooms have clay partition walls and triple-glazed windows to store heat and moderate the room temperature. Heating is provided by a biomass plant that is fuelled by carbon-dioxide-neutral wood chippings gathered from the surrounding forest and adds yet more eco-credibility to the resort.

Vigilius doesn't set out to be just eco-friendly: it has a determined holistic philosophy that matches the most ardently spiritual spas. There is a mantra of evolving new energy, of understanding humanity through the observation of nature, and of an uncluttered 'openness' that will lead to insight. This informs a design that has external linearity and an emphasis on glass and simple interiors: the library, indoor pool and bedrooms benefit from an uninterrupted view of the mountains through

Above: **Vigilius, South Tyrol.** The facade of the building is mostly larch wood and glass, sitting amongst the trees 1,500 metres up on the Vigiljoch mountainside

Opposite: **Vigilius, South Tyrol.** The building slopes outwards at one end, giving it an organic form. As much of the exterior is glazed, horizontal wooden slats are used to prevent the sun overheating the rooms

Hotel name	Vigilius Mountain Resort
Address	Vigiljoch, 39011 Lana, Südtirol, Italy
Telephone	+39 0473 556 600 or design hotels™ 00800 37 46 83 57
Website	www.vigilius.it
Design style	Organic architecture – nature and architecture blur in a wooden cabin in the heavens
No. of rooms	35 rooms, 6 suites
Bars and restaurants	1500 restaurant for the modern gourmet, Ida for traditional South Tyrolean
Spa facilities	Panta Rei spa: wide range of facilities and treatments including Kneipp cold water baths, sauna, indoor pool, reflexology, massages, Shiseido treatments, manicures, pedicures, depilation, facials and solarium
Clientele	International gathering point for artistic, philosophical and spiritual nature-lovers

huge amounts of glazing, while inside the rooms, the clay partition is the only internal wall, which provides some privacy in the bathroom. However, any leanings towards minimalism are 'warm'. Vigilius does not come across as a place for browbeating and birching, but attempts to offer a balance between comfort and contemplation. The reception immediately lets it be known that this is a social place as it doubles as a comfortable lounge, with burgundy leather chairs, long sofas and red carpets enhancing the warmth of the wooden floors and walls. The building has several other social foci, including two restaurants and the Piazza, named after the traditional heart of the Italian town where news is shared and friendships are rejoined. Variations of deep-coloured natural materials, large sofas and masses of cushions temper the coolness of stone.

Vigilius's Panta Rei spa enjoys a high priority in this traffic- and stress-free natural setting. The design of the spa, which includes nine treatment rooms, the pool, a sauna and a meditation room, lends itself to greater minimalism than the rest of the resort. All the areas are simple and sparse, with an emphasis on natural materials and, where possible, unobstructed views of real nature. Beleaguered jet-setters and stressed-out urbanites can restore an inner calm, while still benefiting from the luxury

of individualism which probably fuels so much of their metropolitan lives. Described as 'applied Kiniesiology', the methodology of the spa is to devise an utterly personal system of treatments based on 'a mind and body feedback system'. I think that might be a convoluted way of saying that you shouldn't be doing something if it hurts, which strikes me as a thoroughly good vacation philosophy.

Right and below: Vigilius, South Tyrol. The room design is simple and uncluttered but, as with most of the hotel's interiors, warm burgundies and browns are used to add an element of luxury and prevent the look becoming too spartan

Opposite: Vigilius, South Tyrol. The use of natural materials and colours is a feature of all the rooms, as is the floor-to-ceiling glazing which provides a continual contact with the natural surroundings. The clay partition on the right is used to store and slowly release heat, while also dividing the main area from the bathroom in the otherwise open-plan design

Opposite: Vigilius, South Tyrol. The use of stone and pale wooden floors, along with the wood-clad walls, could lead to an overly cool, minimalist design, but the reception lounge is broken up with the dark hues of comfortable armchairs, sofas and rugs

Left and below: Vigilius, South Tyrol.
The resort has a formal gourmet restaurant, called 1500 to reflect its altitude, and Ida, which serves traditional Tyrolean fare in more rustic surroundings

Left: Vigilius, South Tyrol. Fittingly, the design is at its most sparse in the spa. The meditation room provides few distractions

Below: Vigilius, South Tyrol. The terrace provides a spectacular mountain view for sun-loungers

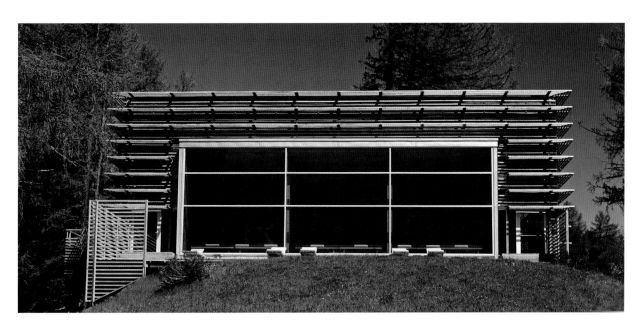

Above and below: **Vigilius, South Tyrol.** The mountain views are uninterrupted for users of the indoor swimming pool

North Island

Silvio Rech &
Lesley Carstens/LIFE &
Virginie Dalais

Location: **Seychelles**
Completion date: **2003**

North Island, the epitome of 'barefoot luxury', is an eco-resort that goes far beyond the ambitions of zero-impact tourism: it plays an active part in changing the environment for the better. The island, packed with its own indigenous flora and fauna, was more or less abandoned in the 1970s with the collapse of the local coconut trade. Free of management, imported plants and species began to wipe out the local varieties and threaten the biosphere. The new owners bought the island with the intention of turning it into a sanctuary for both guests and nature, infusing the project with a philosophy of regeneration and restoration of the natural habitat. During the redevelopment, which was done with the advice of government environmental agencies and ecologists, many threatened species have been preserved while others, including badamier and coco de mer palm trees, tortoises and several bird species, have been carefully reintroduced.

The architecture and interior design is born out of this spirit. Silvio Rech and Lesley Carstens lived on the island with their children as they drew up the plans for architecture which would celebrate the natural environment. The aggressive alien vegetation and dead wood was cleared from the island, but even this found a place within their designs. Takamaka trees, which had died from wilt disease, were used in the main construction and for details such as handrails and screens, while casuarina trees – one of those damaging foreign strains that were cleared from the site – have been reborn as dining tables and library shelves. Many of the other materials, including sandblasted pine, cluciana-wood poles, granitic rock and sandstone, were drawn from other Seychelles islands and southern Africa.

The resort (which is managed by Wilderness Safaris) is made up of 11 stand-alone two-bedroom villas, each covering 450 square metres, and a communal 'piazza' including a library, dive centre, bar, lounge and dining area. Most of the thatch-roofed villas, which have been handcrafted by Seychellois and southern African craftsmen using local stone, wood and glass, follow the treeline so that they are incorporated into the natural setting, while two others are hidden by a takamaka forest. All have good views of the sea and nearby beach.

The interiors, by South African firm LIFE and Virginie Dalais of Mauritius, are sympathetic to Rech and Carstens' 'naturalised' architecture, with the use of largely natural materials and colours. The main colours are white and sand, as befits a beachside resort, amongst a range of polished and weathered woods. The scale of the villas allows for oversize, elongated desks and grand beds made from banuas wood. The living-room furniture includes a large white sofa, a narrow mahogany table with sloping supports and sandstone side tables. Modern furniture, such as classic white Panton chairs, has been incorporated amongst teak and bamboo armchairs. Teak floors add a luxurious lustre. As well as indoor and outdoor showers, the bathrooms feature large rectangular baths sunk into the floor and sliding doors that can be retracted to provide an unbroken open-air view. If bathing proves to be

Above: **North Island, Seychelles.** The glass doors of the villa bedrooms are retractable, allowing an unrestricted view of the sea

Opposite: **North Island, Seychelles.** The accommodation is made up of 11 individual thatch-roofed villas close to the beach and sea. The thatch is made from Balinese alangalang grass but resembles latanier, the material used locally

Hotel name	North Island
Address	c/o PO Box 1176, Victoria, Mahé, Seychelles
Telephone	+248 293 100
Website	www.north-island.com
Design style	Back to nature – luxury style
No. of rooms	11 villas
Bars and restaurants	Bar; Seychellois-Creole organic restaurant
Spa facilities	In-villa spa treatments. New spa opens 2005 with treatments made from local ingredients
Clientele	Wealthy, eco-sensitive sun-worshippers and A-list celebs

exhausting in this oasis of relaxation, there is a daybed just beside the tub. Each villa also has a private plunge pool and a shaded deck.

The leaning towards simplicity places extra emphasis on some interesting surprises born out of the use of natural materials. The villas have root-like pergolas while the open, minimalist communal lounge features a large granite boulder supporting one end of a stone counter-top. In the library, which houses a historical archive of North Island and the continuing conservation project, the table is made from a section of casuarina tree suspended from the ceiling by stainless-steel cables. The setting for the bar is also inspired by the distinct fauna of North Island, with takamaka trees, roots and stumps providing much of the décor, while the dining room is set against a wall of granitic rock.

Left: **North Island, Seychelles.** The bedrooms are huge, allowing for a writing area with a long banuas-wood desk and sofa

Below: **North Island, Seychelles.** Furniture in the villa living rooms includes mahogany tables and sandstone side tables. Throughout the resort, the stress is on natural, and often local, materials but departures include classic Panton chairs

Below: **North Island, Seychelles.** The white-
draped beds have banuas-wood frames

Left and below: **North Island, Seychelles.** The most deluxe villa is the Villa Royale, which has a 1.2 x 2 metre sunken bath, but even the normal villa baths are luxurious

Above: **North Island, Seychelles.** The lounge may be a regimented rectangle, but the bar area to the left is a more organic takamaka-tree creation

Top: **North Island, Seychelles.** Natural materials are used to create unusual features, including a stone counter-top supported by a granite boulder and a screen made of coral, in the minimalist lounge

Above: **North Island, Seychelles.** The library features a casuarina tree table-top suspended from the ceiling by stainless-steel cables and a 19th-century anchor found in the bay

Whitepod

Sofia de Meyer

Location: **Villars**
Completion date: **2004**

Skiing may be associated with the thrill-seeking chattering classes who love nothing better than après-ski binging and a blast of the old school song, but there is room for ecotourists up there on the snow-capped mountains, too. Just as well, because if global warming continues at its current rate, it won't be long until the mountains aren't snow-capped at all. On the whole, Europeans aren't very good at eco-resorts, preferring to think of the problem, and tourist responsibility, as something reserved for far-flung places. It takes someone like Sofia de Meyer to wake up and smell the greenhouse gases. Whitepod, her wonderfully simple eco-resort, is situated in the very heart of Europe, above the town of Villars on a Swiss mountainside. Its presence announces that the problem is right here, right now, but so are credible and exciting solutions.

Whitepod is for genuine lovers of nature, and especially those who like their nature covered in a crisp white layer of snow. It's also for lovers of exclusivity. De Meyer, who was raised amongst the tourist hurly-burly of Villars town, has created a sustainable, calm and very personal vacation experience. Its eco-credentials are immediately set out by its inaccessibility. There are no cars, buses or trains to the resort – guests reach it on snowshoes or skis while their luggage is taken by snowmobile. Five two-person tents, or 'pods' as they are called, are arranged around a permanent structure, the restored Chalet Taillevent, which dates from the 1820s. Not only are the tents a zero-impact solution, one imagines that they allow the new eco-adventurers to feel a direct link to the ancient nomads.

The pods are approximately 2.5 metres high by 5 metres across and fixed on a raised wooden platform that also helps to keep the firewood dry. The platform is used as a private terrace for the guests to absorb the stunning scenery of the surrounding mountains. Inspired by the 1950s designs of Buckminster Fuller, the pods are geodesic – the outer material is stretched to take the shortest line between two points on a curve, so that the dome is actually made up of a series of triangular planes (in this case supported by a frame of 2.5-centimetre-wide galvanised steel rods). As a result, as little material as possible is used to enclose the space, while the structure is strong enough to remain standing and resist the elements without the aid of internal supports. The domes are particularly suitable for Whitepod, as they can withstand a snowfall of 220 kilograms per square metre of material, while the minimal surface area makes the design energy efficient … and they also look like igloos. The triple-insulated Army Duck cotton skin is white, so the pods blend into the snow setting.

You're not going to wake up in a Whitepod and think you're in a suite in the Ritz. The luxury is in the rarity of the experience, the chance to walk and ski within an untouched wilderness rather than trample over it. Nevertheless, the pods come with iPods, while warm comforts are provided by organic bedding, woollen throws, and, crucially, a wood-burning stove which is kept fuelled while the guests are out on their jaunts or relaxing in the chalet. The connection with nature is always current, as the design incorporates a 1.5-by-4-metre clear vinyl window. There are no in-tent toilet

Above: **Whitepod, Villars.** Interior of one of the five pods. The design allows for the absence of internal supports, freeing up the space for a double bed. Vinyl portholes and a bay window provide constant views of the surrounding mountainside

Opposite: **Whitepod, Villars.** The accommodation consists of five two-person geodesic domes, inspired by the designs of Buckminster Fuller. The pods are fixed onto individual wooden terraces

Hotel name	Whitepod
Address	Near Villars, Vaud Canton, Switzerland
Telephone	+41 (0)79 744 62 19
Website	www.whitepod.com
Design style	Space-age eco-pods
No. of rooms	5 domed tents
Bars and restaurants	Lounge and dining room in the chalet
Spa facilities	Masseur available by appointment
Clientele	Snow-loving Greens

facilities other than a chamber pot, so some guests choose to make a dash for the chalet or, if desperate, add a splash of yellow to the all-white outside world. The chalet is the social centre for the guests, housing a lounge with an open fireplace, dining room and library. The cost is all-inclusive, so there is a regular meal-time gathering of guests, who are often friends who have booked en masse.

As well as appeasing the tourist's conscience, Whitepod offers a rarity of experience that can't be found in Villars. The guests can ski straight from their pods to the empty morning slopes before the first ski-lifts strain their way up from the town, but more than this, Whitepod has two professional guides who can take the guests off-piste to explore the untouched mountainside. Snowshoe trails, ice-climbing on the Diablerets glacier, dog-sleigh expeditions and paragliding are also available for adrenalin junkies. De Meyer, who adheres to the World Tourism Organisation's eco-guidelines, has managed to create an invigorating haven that concedes to nature but manages to enhance, rather than diminish, pleasure.

Above: **Whitepod, Villars.** The pods are grouped around a restored 1820s chalet which includes a dining room, lounge, library and bathroom facilities

Top: **Whitepod, Villars.** The eco-resort is 1,700 metres up on a beautiful mountainside above the town of Villars. The domes are able to support the weight of very heavy snowfall and survive winds up to 310 kilometres per hour

Above and right: **Whitepod, Villars.** The interiors are quite basic but an old-fashioned armchair, side table, cowhide rug and wood-burning stove help to create a homely feel

Morgan's Rock Hacienda & Ecolodge

Matthew Falkiner

Location: **Playa Ocotal**
Completion date: **2004**

Westerners may increasingly be holidaying in the remotest parts of the world in search of new experiences, but talk of a trip to Nicaragua is still met with general incomprehension. There may be some mention of 'civil war', 'American imperialism' or 'jungle' but the beauties of this South American country have largely slipped under the globetrotters' radar. The country is shockingly beautiful, with large unspoilt areas featuring a wide variety of indigenous flora and fauna amongst the rainforest, volcanoes, lakes and beaches. However, a murmur has begun, not least because of the 2004 opening of the acclaimed eco-resort Morgan's Rock in Playa Ocotal, and it will not be long before Nicaragua is talked of as 'the new Costa Rica'. One can only hope that new ventures will meet the demand with the elegance, pride and ethical sensitivity of Morgan's Rock.

The eco-resort is very much 'of' Nicaragua. As the designer says, 'The architecture should be experiential … coming out of the wildlife of the place, being inspired by it and, as much as possible, hiding within it.' It is surprising to find that the designer of this detailed celebration of Nicaraguan nature, materials and culture is a Yorkshireman who fled from designing shopping centres. Matthew Falkiner has been in the country for ten years, and his experience has been at an involved and textural – rather than touristic – level. He runs architecture and furniture firm Simplemente Madera (Just Wood) and the resort is situated within a privately owned forest which was bought by the French Ponçon family, his business partners, as a sustainable source of tropical woods. The resort idea emerged after the Ponçons applied for a free tourism feasibility study from the World Bank. To their horror, the consultant suggested building a

five-star hotel and golf course. This seems to have crystallised the Ponçons' feelings for the ecology of Nicaragua: instead of following the World Bank's advice, they planted thousands of new trees and decided to create an eco-resort.

Falkiner was able to get to know the outstanding Playa Ocotal site, with its divine beach and bay, for two years before commencing the design. The result is a scattered group of 15 bungalows set into the hillside and a hacienda, including a pool, bar and restaurant, which is reached by a 110-metre wooden suspension bridge. The bungalows are given natural privacy by the surrounding forest, but look outwards towards the bay and the expanse of the Pacific Ocean. They have thatched roofs, helping them to blend into the setting, and benefit from the indoor/outdoor style that works so well for nature-lovers, including private outdoor showers and, in some cases, trees growing through the roof. One of the highlights is the covered outside terrace featuring a reclining, hanging daybed. From here, one can see the troupes of howler monkeys that regularly pass by.

The structure is almost entirely wooden, with walnut and jatoba drawn from managed local logging sources and sandblasted eucalyptus posts from a reforestation site. Inside, virtually everything is designed by Falkiner and crafted by local artisans from sustainable or reclaimed materials, including canvas walls and tobacco-plant shades. The depth, quality and polish of the materials give the simple interiors a refined, warm sumptuousness. Almond tree is used for the flooring, with laurel doors and window frames and mahogany details,

Left and Opposite: **Morgan's Rock, Playa Ocotal.**
The eco-resort is designed to have as little impact on the natural beauty of Playa Ocotal as possible. The use of wood and thatch help incorporate the 15 stand-alone bungalows into the forest

Hotel name	Morgan's Rock Hacienda & Ecolodge
Address	Playa Ocotal, near San Juan del Sur, Nicaragua
Telephone	+506 296 9442
Website	www.morgansrock.com
Design style	Handcrafted eco-lodges
No. of rooms	15 bungalows
Bars and restaurants	Organic restaurant serving Central and South American, French and Asian cuisines; bar
Spa facilities	None
Clientele	Adventurous ecotourists tired of Costa Rica's increasing commercialisation

while the supporting walls are made from hand-hewn volcanic stone. The furniture includes an inviting white-linen-covered bed beneath a hand-painted picture of turtles, which lay their eggs in the white sands of the nearby beach.

There is an impressive range of nature-oriented tours with names such as 'The Magic of Reforestation', 'The Dry Forest Experience' and 'The Riverbed Nature Walk'.

There is no shortage of excursions, comfort or luxuries for the guests, but at its heart, Morgan's Rock is a conservation project. It covers 1,800 hectares and has involved the planting of 1.5 million trees, the reintroduction of animal species, the protection of wildlife, and the initiation of sustainable agriculture. Golfers can head elsewhere.

Above: Morgan's Rock, Playa Ocotal. The large bathrooms include two basins with taps handmade from copper tubing

Left: Morgan's Rock, Playa Ocotal. The bungalow interiors feature woods from local sustainable sources. Matthew Falkiner has designed the furniture, including the king-size bed which is adorned with a hand-painted picture of turtles

Below: Morgan's Rock, Playa Ocotal. The 110-metre suspension bridge, connecting the hillside bungalows to the hacienda, is one of the construction's major achievements

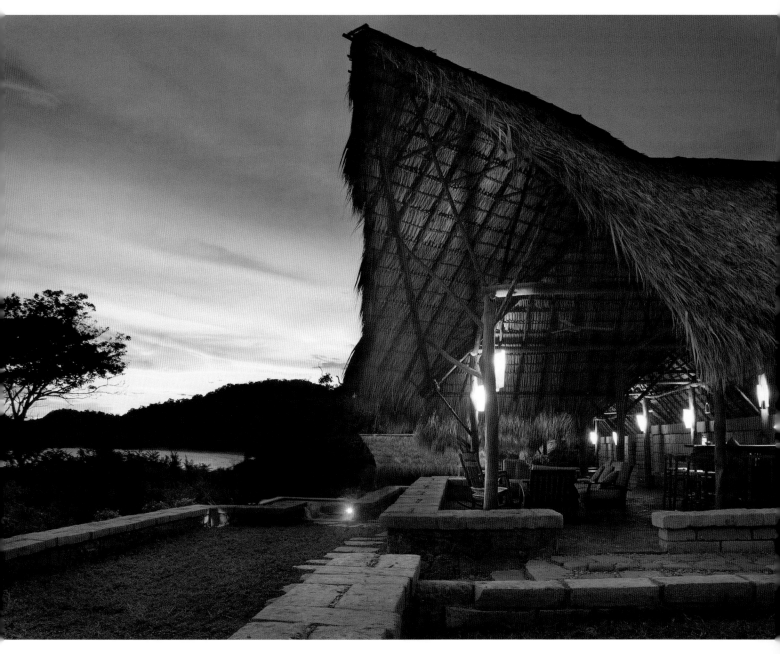

Above: **Morgan's Rock, Playa Ocotal.** The hacienda houses the communal amenities including the bar with a thatched roof partially supported by tree branches

Right: **Morgan's Rock, Playa Ocotal.** The bungalow cabins are raised on stilts so that the buildings interfere with ground-level wildlife as little as possible

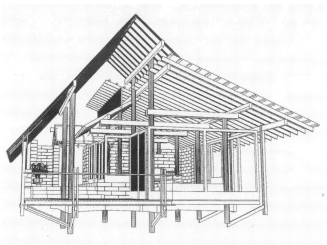

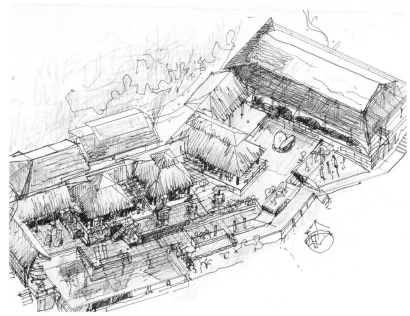

Above: **Morgan's Rock, Playa Ocotal.** Concept
drawing of the hacienda and pool

Left and below: **Morgan's Rock, Playa Ocotal.**
The restaurant overlooks the pool and bay

The Outpost
Daffonchio & Associates

Location: **Kruger National Park**
Completion date: **2002**

The Outpost is one of Africa's most successful examples of an ecologically and culturally responsible tourism venture which also has the benefit of good design and a beautiful, remote setting. It lies in the Makuleke region at the northern edge of the Kruger National Park, 120 kilometres from the nearest town. The Makuleke people had good reason to fear any South African venture, as they had been forcibly removed from their land under apartheid laws in 1969, when the government pushed the Park boundaries north towards the Zimbabwe and Mozambique borders. After the end of apartheid, the Makuleke reclaimed the rights to the region, but agreed that it could remain part of the Park and be used for a small amount of ecotourism. The Outpost was the first venture in the region, so the pressure was on designer Enrico Daffonchio to deliver a lodge that was extremely sympathetic to both the land and its people. To do this and earn awards and recommendations from *Wallpaper**, *Style* and *Condé Nast Traveller* magazines is no small achievement.

The Outpost has an unpretentious, clean and contemporary design using steel, aluminium and canvas. There are 12 individual lodges that run along a hill-path overlooking the Luvuvhu River. Normally, hotel luxury is found within: it forms a protective, exclusive and comforting bubble. In ecotourism, the luxury is found by looking outwards, breaking through the facade and blending the rooms with the natural world as much as possible. At The Outpost, where possible, permanent walls have been done away with: the facades have retractable screens providing a minimum of 180-degree views of the river and valley. The interaction with nature is perhaps at its best in the bathrooms. The vista, which stretches as far as Mozambique, is unbroken from the egg-shaped concrete bath and open shower. The Kruger National Park forms part of the huge Great Limpopo Peace Park and the lodges at The Outpost are very peaceful places. They are simply designed, with much of the furniture, including the king-size bed and a sublime arching double lounge-chair, positioned for the best views. There is also a kiaat-wood desk featuring tusk-shaped legs and, outside the lodges, private divans for quiet contemplation of the wilderness.

Solitude, though, is optional. Meals can be served in rooms, but The Outpost does have a communal dining room, lounge, swimming pool and library (which includes an internet terminal) on a long terrace. The style is contemporary African, with an emphasis on relaxation. In the lounge, there are Nguni cowhides on the cubic poufs and bright, colourful pillows on divans, along with more traditional, upright armchairs. The décor also features a series of works by South African artists including Helen Sebidi, Simon Stone and Beezy Bailey in the dining room, which flows into the lounge. A wine cellar of 3,000 bottles is housed behind a very contemporary glass partition. The polished concrete flooring of the indoor area gives way to wooden decking on the pool terrace, where there are elegant daybeds with roll cushions in the same striped blue material as the lodge divans.

The principal building materials are modern, and not the choice of every designer of eco-lodges, where there is often a leaning towards the use of thatch roofs and woods from local sustainable forests. However, in terms

Above: The Outpost, Kruger National Park. The main building, containing the dining room, lounge and pool, blends into the wilderness

Opposite: The Outpost, Kruger National Park. 12 individual lodges line a hillside walkway over the Luvuvhu River. They are simply designed, with retractable canvas walls ensuring unbroken views

Hotel name	The Outpost
Address	c/o Lodges of Manyaleti (Pty) Ltd, 10 Bompas Rd, Dunkeld West, Johannesburg, PO Box 786064, Sandton 2146, South Africa
Telephone	+27 (0)11 341 0282 or design hotels™ 00800 37 46 83 57
Website	www.theoutpost.co.za
Design style	Modernist enclave in the wilderness
No. of rooms	12 lodges
Bars and restaurants	Restaurant & bar offering Bush cuisine
Spa facilities	None
Clientele	Wealthy international ecotourists

of cultural integration, The Outpost scores high, employing and training the Makuleke people to take over the management of the resort, making sure it is a part of the community rather than an alien intruder. Activities include regular long and short drives for game viewing and trips to the Thulamela archaeological site and a Makuleke village.

Both safari holidays and ecotourism are on the rise, allowing the city slicker to temporarily break away from the stresses and claustrophobia of city life and have a unique and exclusive relationship with nature. However, their popularity is also their downfall: nobody wants to be in a queue of Land Rovers in what is supposed to be the wilderness. For now, the Makuleke Region has been sensitively preserved, while Daffonchio's design ensures that a prized relationship with nature is brought right into The Outpost's lodges in a very stylish manner.

Above, right: The Outpost, Kruger National Park. Panels of African artworks decorate the dining area. The Outpost is proud of its Bush cuisine and has a 3,000-bottle walk-in wine cellar behind a glass partition

Right: The Outpost, Kruger National Park. The lounge features cube seating, covered with Nguni cowhides, upon a polished concrete floor

Left and above: The Outpost, Kruger National Park. The modernist style of the bathrooms makes the utmost of the setting. The Outpost was selected as one of the 'Five Best Baths with a View' by *The Independent* in 2004

Above: The Outpost, Kruger National Park.
Computer rendering of the lounge and bar area.
Enrico Daffonchio has used steel, concrete and
canvas to minimise the barrier between living
spaces and the natural environment

Left and below: The Outpost, Kruger National
Park. The slim outdoor pool is set into wooden
decking at the end of the lounge. Dinner is often
served outside by the pool

retreat and refresh

One of the major shifts in the expectations of hotel culture has been the reintegration of the spa. For this revival, 'taking the waters' has turned into a complex microworld where treatments, atmosphere and materials are combined to offer a serenity that goes beyond physical welfare. The association of spas and physical health has been around since the Babylonian era and became a mainstay of Roman life. The word 'spa' probably derives from the town of Spa in Belgium, whose baths have been popular since the Roman Empire. In Europe, the late 19th and early 20th centuries saw spas reach a new height of popularity, becoming one of the major purposes of travel for the wealthier classes before interest all but dissipated in the post-war period. They have returned, repackaged as a valve for the stresses of urbanity rather than just a place for traditional water cures. The spa is now an expected feature of new hotel design.

So much importance is placed on the psychological and spiritual reaction to the new hotel spa environments that they are part sanatorium, part mental therapy centre and part monastic retreat. As well as providing the traditional ideas of luxury, the hotel has become the portal to both physical and mental wellbeing. Another traditional function – that of offering an escape – is called into question. The guests may be escaping urban pressures, the rat race or destabilising environments, but so many of them are on a quest to find what they regard to be the 'real' person, stripped of the confusions of contemporary life. Rather than running away, the holiday-maker seems to want to find the right mechanisms to help them run back towards an essential idea of themselves. This 'escape to reality' is a revolutionary axis for hotel design. The spirituality of modern spa culture is endlessly emphasised by the location of the hotels and their architectural language, which often draws on Eastern religions. The Bulgari Hotel in Milan is beautifully luxurious, but the

retreat and refresh

luxury is found in a Zen-minimalist design rather than the decorous ostentation one would expect of the Bulgari brand. Spiritual reflection seems as key as the spa treatments in the hotel's evocation of a haven of wellbeing. The religiosity of the experience is further emphasised by the incorporation of the facade of an old convent into the hotel, which also makes much of the convent's peaceful gardens. Uma Paro, which features a Shambhala spa, is situated in the Buddhist kingdom of Bhutan, where the setting, as well as the Ayurvedic techniques, is meant to instil an inner calm. Philippe Starck, meanwhile, draws inspiration directly from heaven for the Agua Bathhouse at the Sanderson in London, and carries the idea of an ethereal retreat from the metropolis through to all areas of the hotel.

The ability to integrate the spa with the rest of the hotel is paramount. The most successful spa hotels often have a holistic approach to design as well as mind, body and spirit. Integration of spa facilities is a particularly difficult challenge for the new breed of country house hotels that are springing up across the UK. Often set in old manor houses but with an emphasis on contemporary interiors, these hotels are a very British retreat from the stresses of city life. They particularly appeal to a style-cognisant breed of media mafiosi, execs and celebs whose careers depend on burning the candle at both ends. Periodically, they need to wholly withdraw from their usual environment in order to survive. The new retreats cushion the withdrawal, offering super-luxury and design delights amongst the fresh air and health-orientated facilities. There is a temptation to see them all as sub-Babington, which opened in 1999 and offered the original, or perhaps just the most noteworthy, contemporary/historical juxtaposition in a country retreat. However, closer inspection reveals many different types of executions and motives, even if they express a common idea. Part of their charm is that they provide an historical certainty, while playing with the design literacy of the guests. Ushida Findlay has moved the concept of the country house residence into the 21st century with plans for Grafton New Hall, a stunning starfish building in the Cheshire countryside. It will be very interesting to see whether British architects and hoteliers can take the concept of the country hotel retreat more fully into the contemporary vernacular without the crutch of historical certainty.

Below: **Babington House, Somerset.** With interiors by Ilse Crawford, Babington House was set up in 1999 as a country retreat for members of Soho House, the celebrity-laden London club

Sanderson
Philippe Starck

Location: **London**
Completion date: **2000**

Whether you are fond of the expressionistic style of the Philippe Starck-designed Ian Schrager hotels or not, they are undeniably both important and successful. Of course, they were pivotal to the rise of the 'boutique' genre, but they are filled with a genuine vivacity that continues to put their imitators to shame. The Sanderson was the apex of the Schrager/Starck collaboration, and not just because it was completed shortly before the two men went their separate ways. Its success is found in its pre-emption – or conjuring up, even – of the need for anti-homogenous metropolitan oases: the Sanderson's Long Bar helped reinvigorate the hotel bar scene, offering a design-led exclusivity that matched the burgeoning style-oriented cocktail culture, while the 'urban spa' concept seems to be a direct reaction to people's growing awareness of an inner dislocation. Long after 'boutique' becomes a swearword to describe lazy hotel interiors, the Sanderson should remain popular because the design's grand gestures are inhabited by an understanding of individual sensibility.

Spas rose spectacularly in popularity in the late 1990s, but the Sanderson helped introduce a new concept. There were three main categories: the exotic resort, the day spa, and the metropolitan hotel with a tagged-on spa facility. The Sanderson gives over an enormous 930 square metres to its Agua Bathhouse spa, but the concept of physical and spiritual enlivenment carries through the whole design of the hotel from the social spaces to the bedrooms. Previously, this holistic approach had largely been confined to remote, specialist resorts. Schrager says, 'The words "spa", "health", and "wellness" get tossed around a lot these days, but when we thought about doing a true "Urban Spa" in London, we were serious about not merely paying lip service to this concept. We wanted to do something that's never been done before – to create a completely integrated

environment – one devoted to your physical, emotional and spiritual health …' He has succeeded: the Sanderson's innovative approach has become a standard-bearer for a more thorough approach to metropolitan spa design, preparing the ground (but not the style) for recent ventures such as Antonio Citterio's serene Bulgari Hotel in Milan.

The hotel takes its name from the 1958 building's former resident, the Sanderson fabric company. Many of

Above: Sanderson, London. The Agua Bathhouse spa features an eclectic mix of furniture including 18th-century Italian chairs and stainless steel

Opposite: Sanderson, London. The hotel lobby is a playground for Philippe Starck's juxtaposition of unusual furniture and objects including a stretched chaise longue, a baroque-style gilt armchair, a cubic net of rocks, and Pierre Paulin's 'Tongue' chair

Hotel name	Sanderson
Address	50 Berners Street, London W1T 3NG, UK
Telephone	+44 (0)20 7300 1400
Website	www.sandersonhotel.com
Design style	Pared-down Starck, touched by the heavens
No. of rooms	150 rooms
Bars and restaurants	Long Bar; Purple Bar (usually reserved for guests); Spoon restaurant
Spa facilities	Agua Bathhouse featuring: 14 treatment rooms; meditation beds; chill-out zones; steam room; gym. Services include aromatherapy facials & body treatments, Agua's speciality treatments and pre-natal programmes
Clientele	Artistic and media-types with a smattering of celebs

the building's features, including murals, mosaics and a beautiful stained-glass window by John Piper, have been incorporated into the redesign but, in typical Starck fashion, are contrasted by outsized furniture, multi-ethnic objects and 'shock' items (such as the huge Salvador Dali 'Mae West Lips' sofa in the lobby) that blur the boundaries of art and utility. Taking up two storeys, the Agua spa is huge and comprises 14 all-white treatment rooms. It draws on the heavens for inspiration: the walls are dressed in floor-to-ceiling white drapes while the Louis XV- and Italian-style furniture is all-white, too. Marble and whitewashed wooden floors, etched Venetian mirrors and porcelain basins maintain a balance between sterility and luxury. Although there are many contemporary touches, including stainless steel, outsized pails and undersized tables, this seems to be a bathhouse for the Roman gods.

The combination of ethereality and relatively pared-down style extends to the rest of the hotel. The guestrooms have white walls, white drapes and glass bathrooms, while the furniture includes a white Eames desk chair. A chrome shelf is decorated with silk-screen images of exercise positions, but pleasure and luxury are conjured up by large mirrors and silver-gilt chairs. The rooms have no solid internal walls, giving the guest a sense of spiritual freedom. The lack of internal divisions extends to the social spaces on the ground floor, where the huge lobby flows into the Long Bar. Featuring a 24-metre-long onyx bar counter and high bar stools decorated on the back with a single eye, this is one of the most popular cocktail bars in London. The design manages to pull off the trick of making the bar seem both exclusive and unconstrained. Although it is protected from prying eyes by white drapes on the glazed facade, it is an uninhibited space that also has the benefit of leading through to a well-designed interior courtyard that is perfect for summertime drinking. The indoor/outdoor concept and the use of light, but luxurious, materials allow the 'urban spa' concept to influence even those areas of the hotel that offer a more wayward sense of wellbeing.

Above: Sanderson, London. The 24-hour gymnasium has state-of-the-art apparatus and private fitness trainers

Opposite: Sanderson, London. Ornate suspended mirrors add to the ethereal mood of the Agua Bathhouse

Left: Sanderson, London. The Long Bar has a 24-metre-long, glowing onyx counter. On the back of each bar stool, Ramak Fazel's image of a female eye overlooks proceedings

Above: **Sanderson, London.** The guestrooms have
white and silver linen, and an image on the ceiling
for bedtime contemplation. Floor-to-ceiling drapes
remove the need for interior walls

Opposite: **Sanderson, London.** The
bathrooms are a glass box and feature
Starck-designed fittings including a round
porcelain basin

Hillside Su

Eren Talu

Location: **Antalya**
Completion date: **2003**

Hillside Su, a gleaming white building in Antalya on the southwest coast of Turkey, stands as a symbol of the country's long-held desire to look west in search of economic stability. Caught on the axis between Europe and Asia, the government of Turkey has pursued a goal of taking the predominantly Muslim country into the European Union. Amongst a raft of financial provisions, legal changes and human rights promises, there has been a transformation of facilities that has helped inspire confidence. The five-star Hillside Su is a leading testament of the new Turkey, attracting both holidaymakers drawn to Konyaalti Beach and businesspeople attending events at the Antalya 'Glass Pyramid' Conference and Exhibition Centre just a kilometre away. The hotel, which has an impressive range of spa facilities, pitches itself as a place for 'reflections of purity' and aims to meet 'the alternative expectations of contemporary individuals with its dynamic lifestyle'. In terms of matching some of the new-found concepts of luxury, where reflection and individuality are the regents, it's right on the money.

A proud white concrete block fronted by a clean, long canopy, the exterior provides a pure expression of Western minimalism, evoking the sterility of a purpose-built, high-tech research laboratory or elite private hospital. At night the block glows with a neon display of changing colours – one colour at a time. Both inside and out, the design is as far removed from the kaleidoscope of the Turkish bazaar as possible. In home-grown designer Eren Talu's concept, most of the walls, floors and furniture are white, from the smart reclining loungers on the terrace's white decking to the all-white rooms. As on the exterior, the use of simple colours within this monochrome glare is very striking. The centrepiece of the interior is its lobby atrium, stretching up through the six floors to the full height of the building, with a ceiling mirror extending the impression far beyond. The internal balcony walls and the floor are white, but orange-red neon seeps under a row of rectangular blocks at ground level and from the recesses between the balconies. Talu has designed a coloured light installation that is projected onto six two-metre-wide spinning disco balls that hang down the centre of the lobby. The effect is of a space-age nightclub.

Monochrome, mirrors and grand proportions are the motifs for much of the design, which may place some emphasis on individuality, but not on intimacy. The main Kirmizi restaurant gives up the white theme to be red, from top to toe. The vast space seats 700 on red 'Catifa' chairs at long rows of red tables, upon a red floor. Even the ceiling is red. The theme is only broken up by mirrored columns that could disorientate the customers amongst this red sea. The lounge bar and restaurant also defies normal expectations as diners sit on white 'Bombo' stools along a high communal Corian table that is so long it recedes into the distance.

Except for the self-controlled mood lighting, huge mirrors, and the colourful bloom of a larva lamp, the rooms are all white. The bed, situated between tall Perspex panels that provide the mood lighting, lies on a plinth that stretches out to form the bedside table and a base for the sofa cushions. Even the television, which

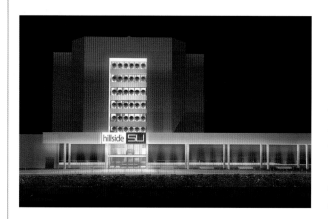

Above: Hillside Su, Antalya. Rendering of the concrete and glass exterior. The white tower is lit with alternating colours. The only other colour is provided by the box trees that decorate the glazing of the atrium facade

Opposite: Hillside Su, Antalya. The enclosed balconies provide an uninterrupted connection between the minimalist hotel rooms and the outside world. The daybeds include their own light source from within the base

Hotel name	Hillside Su
Address	Konyaalti, 07050 Antalya, Turkey
Telephone	+90 (0)242 249 07 00 or design hotels™ 00800 37 46 83 57
Website	www.hillside.com.tr
Design style	Minimalist monochrome meets glitterball glitz
No. of rooms	253 rooms, 41 suites
Bars and restaurants	Lounge, Beach & Pool bars; Kirmizi, Sushi, Beyaz, Lounge, Beach & Pool restaurants
Spa facilities	Indoor & outdoor pools. Six treatment rooms. Steam room, sauna and Turkish bath. Gym. Wide choice of massages, body treatments and baths
Clientele	Sun-worshippers, businessmen and minimalists who like a little glitter with their Zen

offers voyeuristic live footage of the poolside and the lobby, is white. On the private balconies, white daybeds, which are underlit like the seating blocks in the lobby, provide uninterrupted views of the Taurus mountains and the sea. This minimalist, monochrome creation is deliberately contrived to provide an uncluttered setting from which to view or reflect upon the world.

The emphasis on spa facilities highlights this intent. As well as indoor and outdoor swimming pools, Hillside Su has a steam room, a sauna and a Turkish bath. There are also a gym and six treatment rooms, together with a calm space made up of white daybeds on a woodblock floor which leads to an exterior equivalent surrounded by flowers. Amongst the exhaustive list of programmes and treatments (caviar firming treatment, anyone?), there is a range of Asian-influenced services including Javanese body scrubs and Balinese Body Polish-Boreh. The design of Hillside Su may look west, but perhaps its spirit looks east.

Below: **Hillside Su, Antalya.** The lounge atrium provides the most stunning architectural feature of the hotel. The ceiling mirrors the six floors while the whiteness is broken up by orange-red neon escaping from between the levels

Opposite: **Hillside Su, Antalya.** The atrium is hung with two-metre-wide mirror balls, reflecting a changing light installation programme that spins above the rectangular lounge seating

Above: Hillside Su, Antalya. In the bedrooms, even the floors and televisions are white. The main source of light comes from tall Perspex panels either side of the bed. The colour can be altered to suit the mood of the guests

Left: Hillside Su, Antalya. A single plinth provides the base for the bed and sofa and acts as a side table. Large mirrors to the side and above the bed enhance an already large space

Opposite, above and below:
Hillside Su, Antalya. Iroko decking surrounds both the indoor and the 50-metre outdoor pools

Above: Hillside Su, Antalya. Smart sun-loungers and large parasols extend the hotel's monochromatic theme to the beach terrace

Below: Hillside Su, Antalya. As well as extensive spa and gym facilities, the hotel has a serene relaxation room filled with daybeds

Above: **Hillside Su, Antalya.** The monochrome theme changes from white to red for the huge Kirmizi restaurant which seats 700 on banquettes and Arper's 'Catifa' chairs

Left and below: **Hillside Su, Antalya.** The lounge restaurant and bar features elongated, altar-like communal tables surrounded by Magis 'Bombo' stools

Uma Paro

Kathryn Kng/ Cheong Yew Kwan

Location: **Paro**
Completion date: **2004**

Understatement, spiritual and mental revival, and quiet comfort seem to be the watchwords for Uma Paro, situated in Bhutan, a Buddhist, Himalayan kingdom virtually untouched by tourism. The resort's developers have walked on tiptoe, attempting to introduce tourism to an insular, rich culture without crassness or domination. The aim is to have the largely Western visitors appreciate, share and gain from Bhutanese values.

Much of Bhutan is an ecologist's heaven where the natural mountain culture has been preserved from development and pollution. Uma Paro, which has 18 rooms, two suites and nine villas, endeavours to be an ecologically and socially sensitive resort, and is committed to developing wild-flower meadows and multi-varietal woodland that will attract more birdlife into the region. The main house, the former residence of a local nobleman, is a timeless traditional building that blends into the hillside setting. The challenge for architect Cheong Yew Kwan was to create the new villas in a style that evoked a Bhutanese village. Placed on different levels, the villas follow the natural contours of the hillside and are dispersed among orchards, lawns and flowering plants. Bhutanese artisans helped construct the villas using traditional techniques to handcraft natural materials.

The interiors are by Kathryn Kng, whose work includes the Metropolitan Bangkok for Como Hotels and Resorts, which runs Uma Paro and its Balinese sister-resort Uma Ubud. The style is quite contemporary, affording typical modern hotel luxury, but the details are locally inspired. The walls and Shesham-wood furniture are decorated with birds and flowers hand-painted by local artists. Bedcovers are hand-stitched with typical Bhutanese motifs and colours while the handwoven rugs are from nearby Nepal. Some of the villas also have traditional *bukhari* fireplaces. The rooms and suites have a subdued elegance, with light colours helping to highlight the carved wooden windows. They are calm spaces, well suited for reflection, with an emphasis on the views of the forest and snow-capped mountains. However, they do house modern conveniences and distractions, including flat-screen televisions, DVD players, oversized bathrooms with heated towel rails, minibars and electronic safes.

The hotel facilities include a restaurant in a circular, wood-and-glass pavilion amongst the Blue Pine trees. The plain wooden chairs and tables are simply arranged around *bukhari* stoves while the largely organic food includes traditional Bhutanese dishes and contemporary takes on other local Asian cuisines. The COMO Shambhala spa is a very important feature of the resort, offering spiritual and physical relaxation for the guests who have sought out this retreat in an effort to restore a sense of mental and physical wellbeing. Highlights include a 90-metre-square hot-stone bathhouse in the forest, a very modernist indoor swimming pool, a yoga room overlooking

Left and above: Uma Paro, Paro. Inside the main building, the guestrooms benefit from the existing carved wooden window frames

Opposite: Uma Paro, Paro. The main building of the hotel is a traditional, former nobleman's house surrounded by a Blue Pine forest

Hotel name	Uma Paro
Address	PO Box 222, Paro, Bhutan
Telephone	+975 8 271597
Website	www.uma.como.bz
Design style	Traditional Bhutanese house and villas
No. of rooms	20 rooms & 9 villas
Bars and restaurants	Bukhari Restaurant serving Bhutanese and Indian cuisine; bar; fresh juice bar at the COMO Shambhala Retreat
Spa facilities	COMO Shambhala featuring 4 treatment rooms; hydropool; indoor pool; hot-stone bath house; gym; yoga room. Holistic therapies including reflexology, Ayurveda, massage and facial treatments
Clientele	Wealthy business people and celebs seeking inner calm and cultural enlightenment without the hair shirt

the Paro Valley and ancient Ayurvedic healing treatments. A further sense of wellbeing lies beyond the confines of the resort, with an emphasis on learning to understand the noble Bhutanese culture through trips to monasteries, festivals, villages and markets, as well as seeing the local environment through guided walks, camping treks and mountain biking.

The Bhutanese are very wary of the pitfalls of tourism, having witnessed its effect on Nepal. Consequently, they have legislated against the disruption of their indigenous culture: the number of visitors allowed into the kingdom is restricted to 8,000 a year, and each must spend at least $200 a day in high season. The result is that only the wealthy can share in Bhutan's cultural riches, but this is the price that has to be paid for conservation. One only hopes that the appeal of tourist income doesn't lead to a lessening of the restrictions or else Bhutan could become overrun by a horde of more disrespectful culture vultures.

Above, left: Uma Paro, Paro. All the rooms, suites and villas have views of the forest, valley or mountains. The interiors are stylish but restrained, with a simple modernism that enhances locally crafted woodwork and detailing

Above: Uma Paro, Paro. Much of the furniture is made from local Shesham wood, including the lobby tables and chairs. The cushions carry traditional Bhutanese colours and motifs

Left: Uma Paro, Paro. The Bukhari Restaurant is housed in a circular wood and glass pavilion, centred on a large stone pillar and traditional bukhari, wood-fed stoves

Above: Uma Paro, Paro. The Shambhala spa treatment rooms may be modern but many of the treatments are ancient, inspired by 3,000-year-old Vedic healing techniques used to restore the body to its natural equilibrium

Left: Uma Paro, Paro. COMO Shambhala spa facilities include a sublimely modernist indoor pool, with graceful, curving sun-loungers that can be taken onto the outdoor terrace

Above and right: Parrot Cay, Turks & Caicos. COMO first brought the Shambhala spa concept to the Parrot Cay resort, which opened in the remote Turks and Caicos Islands in 1999. The combination of privacy, luxury and spa facilities has made Parrot Cay one of the most esteemed resorts in the world

Bulgari Hotel
Antonio Citterio

Location: **Milan**
Completion date: **2004**

Bulgari opened its first hotel in Milan, the style capital of Europe, in 2004. As Bulgari is one of the world's most famous purveyors of exclusive jewellery and watches, maximalists may have hoped for a jewel-laden paean to ostentatious luxury. However, in the hands of Antonio Citterio, the hotel emerged as a beautiful, calm and refined temple to minimalism. As with most buildings that show a leaning towards clarity, linearity and smooth materials, it has been called Zen, but its spirituality is intrinsically connected to the hotel's setting in the gardens of a convent. Both inside and outside, from the guestrooms to the spa, every detail of the design helps to conjure a harmonious refuge from the buzzing industrial city. Citterio calls it 'a consistent design that makes this environment precise and coherent'. This coherency, or purity of purpose, is enabled by the intelligent balancing of materials and textures, and given context by an interior/exterior synthesis.

Adjoining the Botanical Gardens, the hotel is set in its own 4,000-square-metre garden, part of which has been in existence since at least 1305 when it was mentioned in Piero de'Crescenzi's *Liber Ruralium Commodorum*. The garden has been remodelled by Sophie Agata Ambroise as a verdant escape in the heart of Milan. The building draws on history, too, incorporating facades from different eras including part of an 18th-century convent. Faced with white stucco, the main 1950s facade is punctuated by narrow floor-to-ceiling windows with dark-stained oak frames and, at the top, open gallery recesses. The effect is both light and stylishly authoritative, setting the tone for the studied, reposed interior. Tall, mirrored panes on the ground floor reflect the surrounding greenery to create the apparition of looking through a one-dimensional building. The right-hand side of the building incorporates and exhibits the remaining convent facade, which is framed by bronze.

Inside, the communal areas are designed to appeal to the locals. The building may appear to be very privately situated but the indoor/outdoor relationship helps to make the hotel socially inviting. The five-metre-high lobby, framed by the perpendicular, mirrored windows, is

a monochrome delight, with black granite walls and flooring, white sofa and black-and-white chairs. Accessible from the garden, the bar and restaurant – which has become very popular with the beautiful, stylish and wealthy Milanese – has a clean-cut but warm ambience engendered by teak flooring and a black-resin, oval counter. The lounge, dominated by a monumental 15-tonne black Zimbabwe marble fireplace, houses a changing display of contemporary art from the Massimo De Carlo gallery.

The spa features a sublime combination of natural materials, including Vicenza stone cladding, and is centred on a main hall with a long swimming pool. The contemplative Eastern mood is given a touch of

Above and opposite: **Bulgari Hotel, Milan.** Set in a 4,000-square-metre private garden in the heart of Milan, the hotel incorporates a 1950s building as well as the facade of an 18th-century convent. The building is faced with white stucco, while the windows are given definition by dark-stained oak frames and black-granite overhangs

Hotel name	Bulgari Hotel
Address	Via Privata Fratelli Gabba 7/b, 20121 Milan, Italy
Telephone	+39 02 805 805 1
Website	www.bulgarihotels.com
Design style	Serene minimalist reflections in a garden setting
No. of rooms	49 rooms, 8 executive suites, 1 Bulgari suite
Bars and restaurants	Bar and restaurant
Spa facilities	Spa featuring pool, hammam & treatment rooms. Services include ESPA treatments, Ayurvedic treatments and Balinese massages
Clientele	Wealthy tourists, business people and opera-lovers (it's close to La Scala) seeking an inner-city retreat. The local 'beautiful people' frequent the bar & restaurant

opulence, with gold and emerald mosaic steps leading down into the water. At the end of the pool, a plane of green glass rises up, appearing to reflect the colour of the water. Behind this lies a secluded, peaceful hammam which has seating carved from Turkish Aphyon stone.

Citterio's desire to create an inner-city retreat extends to the heavy bedroom doors which help shut out the noise of the world, so the contemplation of the surrounding gardens can be done in silence. The rooms and suites are light-coloured with natural hues and bleached oak floors, although some of the contemporary Italian furniture and the rugs are dark. The basins and showers are pale Navona travertine stone, while the baths in the standard rooms are black granite. In the Bulgari suite, the monumental bathtub is carved out of a single block of Turkish Bihara stone. The standard rooms tend to be narrow, so the guest moves through a sequence of spaces, but the full-length glazing gives a greater feeling of freedom and enhances the views of the garden. The Bulgari suite, which has a huge Brera stone fireplace, makes the most of the relationship with the garden. The facade is completely transparent, but privacy is ensured as it is wrapped by a three-metre-deep open gallery. The interior teak flooring extends to form the outdoor gallery-terrace so there is a seamless connection with the outside world.

Right, above and below: Bulgari Hotel, Milan.
The executive suites are very gracefully stylised.
Antonio Citterio has designed the furniture
throughout the hotel

Above and below: Bulgari Hotel, Milan. Antonio
Citterio calls the Bulgari Hotel 'an example of total
design'. The serenity of the garden is extended into
the standard guestrooms with the help of natural
hues and materials such as oak and travertine stone

Left: **Bulgari Hotel, Milan.** Emerald-green glass panelling mirrors the colour of the spa's pool and separates the main hall from a private hammam

Above and below: **Bulgari Hotel, Milan.** Minimalism meets exotica: the pool steps are decorated with gold and emerald mosaic. The spa is clad with golden Vicenza stone

Above: Bulgari Hotel, Milan. The lobby, clad with black granite, features black-and-white furniture and tall, narrow windows. It progresses the themes of linear clarity and connection with nature

Right: Bulgari Hotel, Milan. The restaurant and bar has proved to be a hit with the Milanese. Large glass doors open onto the garden, a far corner of which includes the chef's herb and spice garden

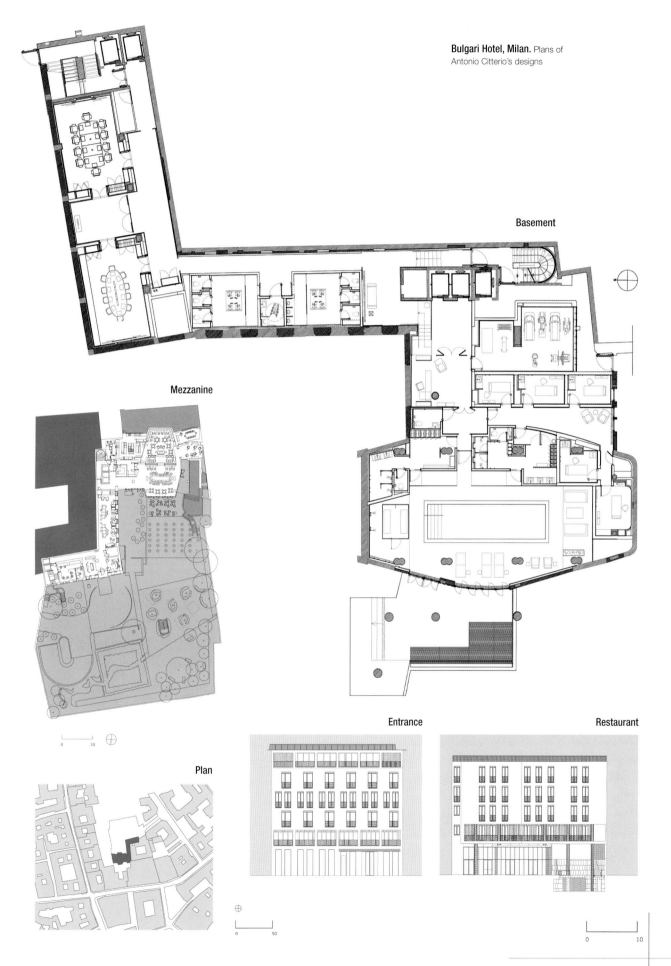

Bulgari Hotel, Milan. Plans of
Antonio Citterio's designs

Basement

Mezzanine

0   10

Plan

Entrance

Restaurant

0   50

0   10

Cowley Manor

De Matos Storey Ryan

Location: **Cowley**
Completion date: **2002**

The names of the room types at Cowley Manor let it be known that the hotel does not intend to be standard: Good, Better, Great, Exceptional and Best. Its high opinion of its facilities, which is reflected in the price (£445 per night for the Best room), is shared, though, by *GQ* magazine which voted it the 'coolest hotel in the world', and it has also figured in *Condé Nast Traveler*'s '50 Hot Hotels'. Amongst the rash of English country retreats, with their history-meets-contemporary makeovers, Cowley Manor does manage to stand out, partly because the architects have introduced excellently resolved elements and partly because the attention to the interiors has been so thorough.

When owners Jessica Sainsbury and Peter Frankopan bought the battered 19th-century manor house, which lies in a beautiful part of Gloucestershire, they turned to their architect friends De Matos Storey Ryan to undertake the transformation of both the structure and the interior. They removed alterations that had disguised the house's former glories and restored it to something akin to its original state, but it is the new departures that are most interesting. The main house and wing are now connected by a stone and glazed enclosure that extenuates some of the original facade detailing but doesn't shy away from looking contemporary. This stylish bravura informs both the conversion of the stable block into guest rooms and the *coup de théâtre* of the project – a sunken outdoor pool and spa building. With a floating roof slicing through the greenery, floor-to-ceiling glazing, and use of rough stone, the spa is slightly reminiscent of Mies van der Rohe's Barcelona Pavilion. While it is linear and modern, it also works well within the landscape of the Grade II*-listed garden. The grounds cover 55 acres with four lakes, a lion-ornamented Victorian cascade, a river and bridges amongst the not overly cultivated terrain. As Cowley Manor has only 30 rooms, it is easy for those guests who are in search of a retreat to feel as if they really have got away from it all.

The interiors benefit from a troupe of specialists, with Kay + Stemmer designing bespoke furniture, Coexistence sourcing a blend of other contemporary and modern classic designs, and Govindia, Hemphill, Tsang creating exclusive fabrics. As a result, even though the historical/contemporary juxtaposition has become a well-worn footprint for country house ventures, Cowley remains distinctly individual. The fabric of the building is allowed to speak for itself, without the need for antique bric-a-brac. Kay + Stemmer's influence is particularly strong in the bedrooms, where much of the furniture is oak, used alongside glass and leather. The kidney-shaped coffee tables and four-poster beds have a particularly striking simplicity. The bedrooms have quite a light, Scandinavian feel, that extends into the bathrooms which feature wooden floors and panelling. The original building's traditional panelling brings a heavy, old-world luxury to the dining room, leavened by the fresh green leather of the dining chairs, also designed by Kay + Stemmer. This green crops up again on walls and furniture covers, and is perhaps drawn from the hotel's pride in its country setting.

To some extent, the interiors provide an exhibition of classic 20th-century furniture designs, but the emphasis

Above: **Cowley Manor, Cowley.** Shelving is built into the sofa-ends in the drawing room

Opposite: **Cowley Manor, Cowley.** The original house, dating from the 17th century, was rebuilt in the Italianate style in the 19th century. It is set in 55 acres

Hotel name	Cowley Manor
Address	Cowley, near Cheltenham, Gloucestershire GL53 9NL, UK
Telephone	+44 (0)1242 870 900
Website	www.cowleymanor.com
Design style	Contemporary luxury – with a citric twist – in an historic setting
No. of rooms	30 rooms
Bars and restaurants	Restaurant; bar; private dining room
Spa facilities	C-Side spa with outdoor pool; indoor pool; treatment rooms. Speciality treatments include Cloud 9 all-over massage and Cor Blimey full body wax
Clientele	Young, hip urbanites

is on user-friendly, comfortable seating rather than grand museum pieces. Items include Arne Jacobsen's 'Egg' chair and ottoman as well as his 'Swan' design, and the Ecart International reissue of Frank and Chanaux's 'Dossier Droit' armchairs, whilst Ron Arad's 'Tom Vac' is used for outdoor areas including the delightful terrace. Elsewhere there are unusual, arresting and humorous objects such as the reception's chandelier made up of hundreds of individually hung crystals, cowhide-covered seats, papier-mâché hunting trophies and a pool room with studded, leather-panelled walls and a blue baize table.

Right and below: **Cowley Manor, Cowley.**
De Matos Storey Ryan architects introduced the new C-Side spa building and outdoor pool into the Grade II*-listed gardens. The modernist complex forms a three-sided sunken courtyard

Above: Cowley Manor, Cowley. The guestrooms feature a combination of modern classic furniture such as Arne Jacobsen's 'Swan' chair, seen by the window, alongside Kay + Stemmer's bespoke designs, including the four-poster bed and kidney-shaped coffee table

Left: Cowley Manor, Cowley. The wood-panelled bathroom has a very Scandinavian feel. The bath and double basins have limestone surrounds, while the mirrored partition hides a walk-through shower

Left: Cowley Manor, Cowley. Kay + Stemmer's lime-green dining chairs give a contemporary edge to the wood-panelled dining room

Left: Cowley Manor, Cowley. Smaller rooms have baths within the main space, but have a private outdoor area featuring Ron Arad's 'Tom Vac' chairs

Above: **Cowley Manor,
Cowley.** The crystal prisms of
a chandelier hang over the
lobby reception area

Right: **Cowley Manor,
Cowley.** Papier-mâché animal
heads look down on the
relaxed bar area

The Grove

Martin Hulbert of Fox Linton Associates/ Fitzroy Robinson

Location: **Chandler's Cross**
Completion date: **2003**

Many of the leaders of the country house hotel revolution have marketed their good transport links with London, emphasising that a retreat from the metropolitan hubbub is only just a couple of hours away. This has been important because so many of the 'retreaters' are London-based executives, media darlings and celebrities. The Grove, the former home of the Earls of Clarendon situated just 40 minutes from the capital, is able to go a step further – or nearer, really – and call itself 'London's country estate'. The house also has the added interest of not just being 'old' in a general but anonymous way: it is historically significant. There has probably been a house on the site since before Elizabethan times, with the 1st Earl of Clarendon taking up residence in the current mansion in 1776. Over the years Horace Walpole, Lord Palmerston, Queen Victoria and Edward VII were all regular visitors to The Grove, which had become known as an ideal place for a weekend in the country, while George Stubbs worked on some of his equestrian portraits there. Since it was sold by the Clarendons in 1920, its residents have been rather less illustrious: it has housed a boarding school, a gardening college and a British Rail training centre.

The Grade II*-listed mansion was bought in 1996 and has been fully restored with English Heritage's approval, while a new west wing has been added by architects Fitzroy Robinson. For the interiors, Fox Linton Associates was hired to reawaken the historical grandeur of the house, returning it to the idyll of the weekend retreat while not stinting on contemporary luxuries. Martin Hulbert, Design Director at Fox Linton Associates, summarises the design approach: 'We wanted to create something that was fantastic but also familiar, almost as though the family had never left the house. Informal luxury – a new take on country house living.' Consequently, the hotel has the layout of a traditional English house, with drawing rooms and a library, but is spurred on by a 21st-century love of pleasure and diversity. These drawing rooms are a great feature of the design, combining luxurious fabrics and comfortable seating with different colour themes and atmospheres. One room has midnight-blue walls and furniture beneath an exuberant blue Murano-glass chandelier. Another blends gold, marble and tassels with 1930s-style seating, a mirror than spreads creeping branches above the fireplace, and a Perspex coffee table. Appreciating the design involves a slow awakening – it takes time to absorb the unusual, contemporary facets within what at first appears to be a traditional room. Against a different backdrop, the artistic, modern oddities would be used as show stoppers; at The Grove they are used as accents to provide depth through subtle, rather than purely brash, juxtapositions. For instance, in some of the bedrooms, the Hulbert-designed four-poster beds are, as expected, dressed in diaphanous folds, but are actually made of Perspex.

The library design does contrive a more obvious shock, separating the central aisle of traditional sofas from the shelving by means of 1.5-metre-tall, curving mirrored panels, while a huge mirror-shield looms over the fireplace. The Grove has three restaurants, each with very different culinary and design flavours. Collette's is

Above: **The Grove, Chandler's Cross.** The reception is housed in the new west wing, where the style is more obviously contemporary. The hotel and gardens host a wide range of art exhibits

Opposite: **The Grove, Chandler's Cross.** The 18th-century mansion, formerly the home of the Earls of Clarendon which was visited by Queen Victoria, is reborn as a country house hotel

Hotel name	The Grove
Address	Chandler's Cross, Hertfordshire WD3 4TG, UK
Telephone	+44 (0)1923 807 807
Website	www.thegrove.co.uk
Design style	18th-century country mansion given multi-textured, high-class overhaul
No. of rooms	216 rooms, 16 suites
Bars and restaurants	Collette's à la carte restaurant; The Glasshouse restaurant and bar; The Stables restaurant & bar
Spa facilities	Sequoia Spa with 13 treatment rooms; therapeutic saline water vitality pool; indoor & outdoor pools; fitness studio; aerobic studio; Jacuzzi; relaxation rooms; ESPA Ayurvedic, holistic and beauty treatments including facials, massages & wraps
Clientele	Burnt-out, luxury-loving Londoners looking for a quick fix

the most formal, offering an à la carte menu in a suave yellow room, decorated with restored 18th-century mouldings and a few contemporary twists. The Stables is suitably more rustic, with an exposed wood setting for a family-oriented menu, while The Glasshouse holds the middle ground. Housed in the new wing, transparency is the theme: it has floor-to-ceiling glass walls and an open kitchen allowing the guests to see the chefs preparing the dishes.

At every turn, The Grove endeavours to emphasise both luxury and individuality through choice. There are three main types of guestroom: the Classic has muted, cool colours drawn from New England style; the Decadent is full of exotic textures including ostrich feathers and sheer, velvet-trimmed drapes, contrasting with the Perspex beds; and the Contemporary rooms in both the mansion and the west wing have cool, natural colours, influenced by the scenic beauty that surrounds the house.

The Grove's style is sometimes described by the owners as 'groovy grand', which is perhaps ill-advised – for me, at least, this conjures up a nightmarish image of an Austin Powers-type character jumping up and down on a Day-Glo-pink piano. Handy though it may be, this shorthand description doesn't do justice to the highly intelligent but intensely pleasurable union of styles that has made The Grove rather beautifully unique in an increasingly over-populated genre.

Left and below: **The Grove, Chandler's Cross.**
One of the drawing rooms brings together chairs fringed with crystal, marble and Perspex tables, and an organic mirror. Elements of the design have survived from the early concept drawings

Right and below: **The Grove, Chandler's Cross.**
Traditional furniture and mouldings are synthesised with contemporary shocks. The sofas are surrounded by tall, mirrored panels that create an inner enclave within the library walls

Above: The Grove, Chandler's Cross. The four
drawing rooms include a midnight-blue lounge
featuring a Murano-glass chandelier

Above: The Grove, Chandler's Cross. One of the New England-inspired Classic guestrooms. Amongst the calm conformity, there is a Perspex four-poster bed and Japanese-influenced screen door

Below: The Grove, Chandler's Cross. The bedrooms of the west wing have a cool, contemporary design, with balconies overlooking the gardens or golf course

Below: The Grove, Chandler's Cross. Of the three restaurants, Collette's is the most formal. Situated in the mansion, its 18th-century mouldings have been restored

Above and right: **The Grove, Chandler's Cross.**
The historic/contemporary blend of the mansion house is foregone in the more minimalist Sequoia Spa designed by Collett Zarzycki

Whatley Manor

Alix Landolt/
AdP Decoration/
No Twelve Queen Street

Location: **Malmesbury**
Completion date: **2003**

Like most of the leaders of the English country house hotel revival, Whatley Manor blends the heritage of the architecture with contemporary flashes, but its approach is very subtle and infused with intelligence at every turn. It benefits from the precision of its Swiss owner, Christian Landolt, and his mother Alix Landolt who has personally overseen the interior design. She has worked alongside the excellently named Dominique Couture from the Swiss company AdP Decoration while Carole Roberts of Number Twelve Queen Street has designed the spa, cinema and boardroom.

The legend of Whatley Manor – a converted Cotswolds hunting lodge based around a courtyard – is 'peace … elegance … quiet luxury'. It is a very carefully contrived retreat from the busy bluster of contemporary lifestyles, and little is rushed. It took two men a year to build the dry-stone wall that runs the length of the drive. As with the most ardent of contemporary designs, the hotel offers an antidote to homogeneity, but it does this through understated luxury rather than shock and surprise. As Alix Landolt says, 'Above all else, I wanted Whatley Manor to feel like a home rather than a hotel, and to exude comfort and warmth whilst still being very stylish.' A home-from-home is the opposite to the ideal of many contemporary designers, who wish their hotels to be an 'event' or a crucible of experiential theatre. Curiously, the route to such different ends is quite similar, with an emphasis on commissioned furniture and contemporary art installations. The Manor is not showy, but it is unique.

The 15 rooms and eight suites have been individually designed, with a blend of antiques and contemporary features, including walls covered with suede by Carlucci di Chivasso, wallpaper by Nina Campbell and fabrics by the likes of Rubelli and Manuel Canovas. Furniture includes pieces by Forestier and John Hutton, while the bathrooms have Philippe Starck-designed tubs and curved Radiance shower units by Matki Showering. The result is ageless and comfortable, and every element, including the Bang & Olufsen Beocenter 1 sound and vision system, is seamlessly integrated. The rooms suit the manor house style, but they are not typically English,

perhaps owing more to upper-class French country style than anything else.

Of the two restaurants, Le Mazot is the less formal and is a far cry from the usual expectations of a country house hotel. Its Swiss chalet style is Whatley Manor's greatest reminder of the owner's origins, but the bar does have a sleek, contemporary edge to it. The more formal Dining Room has won head chef Martin Burge a Michelin star. The hotel also has a Lounge Bar and a terrace that overlooks the gardens, which are one of the hotel's treasures. Based on the original 1920s design, they have been developed into 26 'rooms', ensuring that every guest can enjoy outdoor privacy. Other facilities include a comfortable, dark and luxurious private cinema which has red suede walls and Italian leather seats.

The award-winning Aquarias Spa is sublime and sophisticated with its range of facilities and treatments enhanced by the use of polished plaster walls, aged walnut, marble, slate, mosaics and chrome. The hydrotherapy bath is a futuristic swirl within a pillared chamber, seemingly influenced by Ancient Rome, but the sparsity is tempered by soft loungers and careful lighting. Any leanings toward a hard contemporariness are reined in: at Whatley Manor, comfort is king.

Above: Whatley Manor, Malmesbury. The bar at Le Mazot, Whatley Manor's informal, Swiss-style restaurant

Opposite: Whatley Manor, Malmesbury. The manor house makes the most of its setting in the Cotswold Hills to offer an exclusive, luxurious retreat

Hotel name	Whatley Manor
Address	Easton Grey, Malmesbury, Wiltshire SN16 0RB, UK
Telephone	+44 (0)1666 822 888
Website	www.whatleymanor.com
Design style	Very refined antique-chique
No. of rooms	15 rooms, 8 suites
Bars and restaurants	Michelin-starred The Dining Room restaurant; Le Mazot restaurant & bar; Lounge Bar
Spa facilities	Aquarias Spa: thermal rooms including Finnish sauna; hydrotherapy pool; La Prairie treatments; massages; mud treatments, solarium; gym
Clientele	Winding-down execs, jet-setters and celebs seeking elegance and privacy

Above: **Whatley Manor, Malmesbury.** The
bathrooms include Philippe Starck washbasins,
bathtubs and mixers, with curved Matki
Showering units

Above: **Whatley Manor, Malmesbury.** The
peaceful Aquarias Spa features a hydrotherapy pool
in which guests can relax on underwater loungers

Right: **Whatley Manor, Malmesbury.** Careful
lighting prevents the spa – the most contemporary
area of the Manor – becoming too harsh an
environment. The spa has a range of thermal rooms
including the Tepidarium

Above: Whatley Manor, Malmesbury. The rooms are understated but luxurious, with antiques blending with bespoke contemporary designs

Above: Whatley Manor, Malmesbury. Each of the rooms and suites is individually designed. Contemporary armchairs blend into the timeless, blue theme

Right: Whatley Manor, Malmesbury. The private cinema has red Italian leather seats and suede-lined walls

Above: Whatley Manor, Malmesbury. The terrace,
with its unusual wicker furniture, provides a view
over the gardens at dusk

Hurst House

Juliet de Valero Wills for Dorset Design

Location: **Laugharne**
Completion date: **1999-2007**

Although Hurst House offers the combination of a country retreat and a private London club, it isn't a disciple of the Babington House/Soho House venture. For a start, the country hotel, set in the Laugharne marshes in a remote part of Wales, opened in the same year as Babington. In style terms, it also shies away from the full-on historic/contemporary juxtaposition that is Babington's often-forged signature. Hurst House has been a slow, organically evolving project that has found its own way of doing things. It is finally taking the expected, but expensive, leap towards providing spa facilities as part of a proposed expansion. Originally, the plan was for a unique, ecologically friendly, earth-covered mound housing a complex shaped like a nautilus shell but this ambitious project has since been modified.

As the home of Dylan Thomas, Laugharne is a famous literary destination. The author of *Under Milk Wood* wrote in a boathouse and used to head to Brown's Hotel, which is also owned by Hurst House, for his legendary drinking bouts. Hurst House proper is a former dairy farm lying out of town in 69 acres of marshland that stretches towards the sea. Matt Roberts, who lived on the farm, teamed up with actor Neil Morrissey to create a small hotel – it currently has only six rooms – with the focus on a highly acclaimed restaurant and bar.

The designer, Juliet de Valero Wills, finds themes an anathema. If there is any connection between the individual room designs, it is found in the idea of the Grand Tour – a gathering together of beautiful and interesting objects from different cultures across the ages – but the result is not a contrived eclecticism. It is a warm environment, where modern, reclaimed and antique pieces, including Indian arches and 19th-century beds, work together to create a chic but unpretentious luxury. The house is mainly Georgian, with exposed beams, sash windows and parquet flooring, but the colours, including the orange reception area and blood-red restaurant, are bold. The bar has a clubby feel, with leather armchairs and sofas and moody lighting, while the restaurant has a more contemporary look, with metal table legs and local modern art standing out amongst the artefacts and dark walls. The mood, but

not the design, has been replicated in the Hurst House private club, which opened recently in London. Like the country retreat, it appeals to the media and artistic crowds.

De Valero Wills believes Hurst House should allow guests to 'disappear into a bubble that is different and special'. In recent years, she says that a challenge is 'to raise your game for design literacy': she wants to create an individual interior that even the most design-savvy will not be able to call a home-from-home. Sourcing the right elements, whether modern or reclaimed, has been the key to creating an anti-homogenous, spirited design that nonetheless puts comfort before exhibitionism.

Some of the rooms have interesting architectural solutions to the need to bring modern facilities into an old framework. An en-suite bathroom is housed in a curving, green Wendy house, complete with internal window, which divides the bedroom and sitting area. The heavy textures of cushions and drapes around the dark wooden beds are tempered by the use of lighter, reclaimed furniture and pale carpets.

The popularity of the bedrooms has inspired the planned expansion that will incorporate 23 rooms by sensitively adapting the outer buildings around the house's existing Georgian farmyards. As well as the excellently designed spa, new buildings will cater for a larger bar and restaurant, and a cinema.

Above: Hurst House, Laugharne. Founded as a dairy farm in the 16th century, much of the current Hurst House is Georgian

Opposite: Hurst House, Laugharne. The acclaimed and popular restaurant has blood-red walls and is dressed with a wide range of antiques, artefacts and modern art pieces

Hotel name	Hurst House
Address	East Marsh, Laugharne, Carmarthenshire, South Wales SA33 4RS, UK
Telephone	+44 (0)1994 427 417
Website	www.hurst-house.co.uk
Design style	A contemporary Grand Tour in a Georgian setting
No. of rooms	6 rooms
Bars and restaurants	Modern British/French restaurant; bar
Spa facilities	Massage and reiki from in-house therapist. Full spa facilities are planned
Clientele	Creatives, media and celebs seeking a country retreat

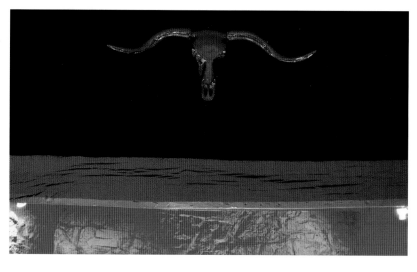

Above and left: Hurst House, Laugharne. The communal areas benefit from the use of strong colours and interesting details, including a silver bull's skull

Below: Hurst House, Laugharne. With parquet flooring, reclaimed wooden tables and leather chairs, the bar has the feel of an old club

Above: **Hurst House, Laugharne.** Huge bolsters and Indian arches above 19th-century dark wooden beds help provide interesting forms and textures. The design draws upon the influence of the Grand Tour, when British aristocrats would cherry-pick artefacts from other cultures

Above: **Hurst House, Laugharne.** The sitting area is divided from the bedroom by a curved, green Wendy house that houses the en-suite bathroom

Left: **Hurst House, Laugharne.** The bathrooms have round, white enamel sinks supported by clear-glass surrounds

design
for living

A directory of some of the classic and contemporary designs, drawn from the *Hotel Revolution* interiors, that are commercially available. Go to the listed websites for further details of the products, showrooms and retail outlets.

Chairs

'Kab' chair by Karim Rashid
Project: Semiramis
Available from: Frighetto
Showroom, via Moneta,
214 - zona Pomari,
36100 Vicenza, Italy
Tel: +39 0444 291020
Fax: +39 0444 283907
www.frighetto.it

'Tom Vac' chairs by Ron Arad
Project: Cowley Manor
Available from: Vitra Ltd, 30 Clerkenwell
Road, London EC1M 5PQ, UK
Tel: +44 (0)20 7608 6200
Fax: +44 (0)20 7608 6201
www.vitra.com

'Little Tulip' chairs by Pierre Paulin
Projects: Hôtel du Petit Moulin, The
Zetter Restaurant & Rooms.
Available from: Artifort, Postbus 115,
NL 5480 AC Schijndel, The Netherlands
Tel: +31 (0)73 658 00 20
Fax: +31 (0)73 547 45 25
verkoop@artifort.com
www.artifort.com

'Egg' chair by Arne Jacobsen
Project: Cowley Manor
Available from: Fritz Hansen
Showroom, 20-22 Rosebery
Avenue, London EC1R 4SX, UK
Tel: +44 (0)20 7837 2030
Fax: +44 (0)20 7837 2040
sales@fritzhansen.com
www.fritzhansen.com

'Swing' chair by Karim Rashid,
Project: Semiramis
Available from: Karim Rashid Shop, 137 West
19th Street, New York, NY 10011, USA
Tel: +1 212 337 8078
Fax: +1 212 337 8515
www.karimrashidshop.com

'Kayak' chairs by Jorge Pensi
Project: Omm
Available from: SARE, Olalde Urrestilla,
20730 Azpeitia – Gipuzkoa, Spain
Tel: +34 943 151110
Fax: +34 943 151120
info@sare.es
www.sare.es

**'Flow' chair designed by Luke
Pearson/Tom Lloyd**
Project: The Zetter Restaurant & Rooms
Available from: Walter Knoll AG & Co.KG,
Bahnhofstraße 25, D-71083 Herrenberg,
Germany
Tel: +49 (0)70 32 208 0
Fax: +49 (0)70 32 208 250
e-mail: info@walterknoll.de
www.walterknoll.de

'VIP' chair by Marcel Wanders
Project: Lute Suites
Available from: Moooi,
Minervum 7003, 4817 ZL Breda,
The Netherlands
Tel: +31 (0)76 578 4444
Fax: +31 (0)76 571 0621
info@moooi.com
www.moooi.com

'Bubble Club' chair by Philippe Starck
Project: Omm
Available from: Kartell at Selfridges, 44
Oxford Street, London W1A 1AB, UK
Tel: +44 (0)20 7318 3791
kartell26@aol.com
For other outlets go to www.kartell.it

Sofas

'Loft' sofa by Lluís Codina
Project: Omm
Available from: Perobell, Avda Arraona 23,
8205 Sabadell, Spain
Tel: +34 93 745 79 00
info@perobell.com
www.perobell.com

'Extra Wall' sofa/day bed
Project: 25hours
Available from: Living Divani, Strada del Cavolto,
Anzano del Parco, Como 22040, Italy
Tel: +39 031 630954
www.livingdivani.it

'Spline' sofas and chairs by Karim Rashid,
Project: Semiramis
Available from: Karim Rashid Shop, 137 West
19th Street, New York, NY 10011, USA
Tel: +1 212 337 8078
Fax: +1 212 337 8515
www.karimrashidshop.com

Tables & desks

'25hours' desk/seat by 3Meta
Project: 25hours
Available from: 25hours, Paul-
Dessau-Straße 2, 22671 Hamburg,
Germany
Tel: +49 (0)40 855 07 0
Fax: +49 (0)40 855 07 100
info@25hours-hotel.com
www.25hours-hotel.com

'Cowley' dining table & chairs
by Kay + Stemmer
Project: Cowley Manor
Available from: Kay + Stemmer,
Oblique Workshops, Stamford Works,
Gillett Street, London N16 8JH, UK
Tel: +44 (0)20 7503 2105
Fax: +44 (0)20 7275 7495
info@kay-stemmer.com
www.kay-stemmer.com

'Aqua' table by Zaha Hadid
Project: Hotel Puerta América
Available from: Established & Sons,
29-31 Cowper Street, London EC2A
4AT, UK
Tel: +44 (0)20 7608 0990
Fax: +44 (0)20 7608 0110
info@establishedandsons.com
www.establishedandsons.com

'Organic' coffee table
by Kay + Stemmer
Project: Cowley Manor
Available from: Kay + Stemmer,
Oblique Workshops, Stamford Works,
Gillett Street, London N16 8JH, UK
Tel: +44 (0)20 7503 2105
Fax: +44 (0)20 7275 7495
info@kay-stemmer.com
www.kay-stemmer.com

Lighting

'Set Up' shade by Marcel Wanders (left)
Random Light by Monkey Boys (middle)
Project: Lute Suites
Available from: Moooi, Minervum 7003,
4817 ZL Breda, Netherlands
Tel: +31 (0)76 578 4444
Fax: +31 (0)76 571 0621
info@moooi.com
www.moooi.com

'Oven 125' lamps by Antoni Arola
Project: Omm
Available from: Santa & Cole, Dolors Granés
32, E 08440 Cardedeu, Spain
Tel: +34 938 462 437
Fax: +34 938 711 767
info@santacole.com
www.santacole.com

'Spun' floor lamp by Sebastian Wrong
Project: 25hours
Available from: 25hoursPaul-Dessau-Straße 2,
22671 Hamburg, Germany
Tel: +49 (0)40 855 07 0
Fax: +49 (0)40 855 07 100
info@25hours-hotel.com
www.25hours-hotel.com

Bathroom

Bathtub, basin, mixers by Philippe Starck
Project: Whatley Manor
Available from: Duravit Starck bathtub and
basin – Duravit AG, Werderstraße 36,
D-78132 Hornberg, Germany
Tel: +49 7833 70-0
Fax: +49 7833 70-289
info@duravit.de
www.duravit.com

Available from: Axor Starck mixers –
Hansgrohe Limited, Unit D1 and D2, Sandown
Park Industrial Estate, Royal Mills, Esher,
Surrey, KT10 8BL
Tel: +44 (0)870 7701972
Fax: +44 (0)870 7701973
info@hansgrohe.co.uk
www.hansgrohe.co.uk or www.axor-design.com

'Gobi' washbasin by Marcel Wanders
Project: Lute Suites
Available from: Boffi Studio Alternative Plans,
4 Hester Road, London SW11 4AN, UK
Tel: +44 (0)20 7228 6460
Fax: +44 (0)20 7924 1164
altplans@dircon.co.uk
http://www.alternative-plans.co.uk
See www.boffi.com for international dealers

Beds

'Morgan's Rock' bed by Matthew Falkiner
Project: Morgan's Rock
Available from: Simplemente Madera, Nicaragua
Tel: +505 270 1804
exchange@ibw.com.ni
www.simplementemadera.com

'Cowley' four-poster bed by Kay + Stemmer
Project: Cowley Manor
Available from: Kay + Stemmer,
Oblique Workshops, Stamford Works,
Gillett Street, London N16 8JH, UK
Tel: +44 (0)20 7503 2105
Fax: +44(0)20 7275 7495
info@kay-stemmer.com
www.kay-stemmer.com

Surfaces

Marmoleum 'Real 3127'
Project: Q!
Available from: Forbo Flooring, Forbo Nairn Ltd,
PO Box 1, Kirkcaldy, Fife KY1 2SB, UK
Tel: +44 (0)1592 643 777
Fax: +44 (0)1592 643 999
www.forbo-flooring.co.uk

Mosaic tiles by Bisazza
Project: Hotel on Rivington
Available from: Bisazza, Viale Milano 56,
36041 Alte Vicenza, Italy
Tel: +39 0444 707511
Fax: +39 0444 492088
www.bisazza.com

Hotel listings

Argentina

Faena Hotel + Universe

Martha Salotti 445

Buenos Aires C1107CMB

Tel: +54 (0)11 4010 9000

www.faenahotelanduniverse.com

Bhutan

Uma Paro

PO Box 222

Paro

Tel: +975 8 271597

www.uma.como.bz

France

Hôtel du Petit Moulin

29-31 rue du Poitou

75003 Paris

Tel: + 33 (0)1 42 74 10 10

www.paris-hotel-petitmoulin.com

Germany

Q!

Knesebeckstrasse 67

10623 Berlin

Tel +49 (0)30 810066 0

www.q-berlin.de

25hours

Paul-Dessau-Straße 2

22671 Hamburg

Tel: +49 (0)40 855 070

www.25hours-hotel.com

Greece

Semiramis

48 Charilaou Trikoupi Street

145 62 Kefalari – Kifissia

Athens

Tel: +30 210 62 84 400

www.semiramisathens.com

Italy

Aleph

Via di San Basilio 15

00187 Rome

Tel: +39 06 422 901

www.boscolohotels.com

Bulgari Hotel

Via Privata Fratelli Gabba 7/b

20121 Milan

Tel: +39 02 805 805 1

www.bulgarihotels.com

Vigilius Mountain Resort

Vigilioch

39011 Lana

Südtirol

Tel: +39 0473 556 600

www.vigilius.it

The Netherlands

Lute Suites

Amsteldijk Zuid 54-58

1184 VD Ouderkerk a/d Amstel

Tel: +31(0)20 47 22 462

www.lutesuites.com

Nicaragua

Morgan's Rock Hacienda & Ecolodge

Playa Ocotal

near San Juan del Sur

Tel: +506 296 9442

www.morgansrock.com

Seychelles

North Island

c/o PO Box 1176

Victoria

Mahé

Tel: +248 293 100

www.north-island.com

South Africa

The Outpost

c/o Lodges of Manyaleti (Pty) Ltd,

10 Bompas Road

Dunkeld West

Johannesburg

PO Box 786064

Sandton 2146

Tel: +27 (0)11 341 0282

www.theoutpost.co.za

Spain

Hotel Puerta América

Avenida de América 41

Madrid 28002

Tel: +34 902 363 600

www.hotelpuertamerica.com

Omm
Rosselló 265
Barcelona 08008
Tel: +34 93 445 40 00
www.hotelomm.es

Switzerland
Whitepod
near Villars
Vaud Canton
Tel: +41 (0)79 744 62 19
www.whitepod.com

Turkey
Hillside Su
Konyaalti
07050 Antalya
Tel: +90 (0)242 249 07 00
www.hillside.com.tr

United Arab Emirates
Burj Al Arab
PO Box 74147
Dubai
Tel: +971 4 301 7777
www.burj-al-arab.com

United Kingdom
Courthouse Hotel Kempinski
19-21 Great Marlborough Street
London W1F 7HL
Tel: +44 (0)20 7297 5555
www.courthouse-hotel.com

Cowley Manor
Cowley
near Cheltenham
Gloucestershire GL53 9NL
Tel: +44 (0)1242 870900
www.cowleymanor.com

Dakota
Lakeview Drive
Sherwood Business Park
Annesley
Nottingham NG15 0DP
Tel: +44 (0)870 442 2727
www.dakotahotels.co.uk

easyHotel
14 Lexham Gardens
London W8 5JE
www.easyhotel.com

The Grove
Chandler's Cross
Hertfordshire WD3 4TG
Tel: +44 (0)1923 807807
www.thegrove.co.uk

Hurst House
East Marsh
Laugharne
Carmarthenshire
South Wales SA33 4RS
Tel: + 44 (0)1994 427417
www.hurst-house.co.uk

Sanderson
50 Berners Street
London W1T 3NG
Tel: +44 (0)20 7300 1400
www.sandersonhotel.com

Whatley Manor
Easton Grey
Malmesbury
Wiltshire SN16 ORB
Tel: +44 (0)1666 822888
www.whatleymanor.com

The Zetter Restaurant & Rooms
86-88 Clerkenwell Road
London EC1M 5RJ
Tel: +44 (0)20 7324 4444
www.thezetter.com

United States of America
Hotel on Rivington
107 Rivington Street
New York
NY 10002
Tel: +1 212 475 2600
www.hotelonrivington.com

Metronaps
Empire State Building
350 Fifth Avenue
New York
NY 10118
Tel: +1 212 239 3344
www.metronaps.com

QT
125 West 45th Street
New York
NY 10036
Tel: +1 212 354 2323
www.hotelqt.com

Further Reading

Books

Ultimate Hotel Design, editor Aurora Cuito, teNeues (London), 2004

New Hotels, Alejandro Bahamon, Harper Design International (New York), 2003

Bar Style: Hotels and Members' Clubs, Howard Watson, Wiley-Academy (Chichester), 2005

New Hotel: Architecture and Design, David Collins, Conran Octopus (London), 2001

Luxury Hotels Europe, Martin N Kunz, teNeues (London), 2003

New Hotels for Global Nomads, Donald Albrecht, Merrell (London), 2002

Hotel Design, Planning and Development, Walter A Rutes, Richard H Pinner, Lawrence Adams, WW Norton (New York), 2001

Tourism and Hospitality in the 21st Century, editors S Medlik & Andrew Lockwood, Butterworth Heinemann (London), 2002

Hotel Interior Structures, Eleanor Curtis, Wiley-Academy (Chichester), 2001

Periodicals & Magazines

Sleeper, Mondiale Publishing (Stockport)

Domus, Editoriale Domus SpA (Milan), particularly the 'Hotel Extra' supplement to Vol 864, Nov 2003, editor Deyan Sudjic, and the 'Travel Settings' supplement to Vol 875, Nov 2004, editor Stefano Casciani

FX, ETP (Chelmsford)

Architectural Design, Wiley-Academy (Chichester)

Hospitality Design, VNU (New York)

Hotel Design, Advanstar (New York)

Condé Nast Traveler, Condé Nast Publications (London)

Hotel guides

Hip Hotels series, particularly *Hip Hotels: City*, Herbert Ypma, Thames & Hudson (London), 2002 edition

The Black Book series, particularly *The Black Book List New York 2005: Restaurants, Bars, Clubs, Hotels*, Evan Schindler et al, Black Books (New York), 2004

Mr & Mrs Smith Hotel Collection: UK/Ireland, Spy Publishing (London), 2003

Mr & Mrs Smith Hotel Collection: European Cities, Spy Publishing (London), 2004

Good Hotel Guide Great Britain and Ireland, Desmond Balmer, Ebury Press (London), 2004

The Which? Guide to Good Hotels 2005, Kim Winter, Which? Books (London), 2004